BUMPER

Cadbury
Bourn Vita
Quiz
CONTEST

Quiz Book

Derek O'Brien was born in Kolkata. He began his career as a journalist for *Sportsworld* magazine but soon shifted to advertising. After working for a number of very successful years as Creative Head of Oglivy, Derek decided to focus all his energy and talent in his passion – quizzing.

Today, Derek is Asia's best-known quizmaster and the CEO of Derek O'Brien & Associates. He is the host of the longest-running game show on Indian television, the Cadbury Bournvita Quiz Contest, for which he was voted the Best Anchor of a Game Show at the Indian Television Academy Awards for three years in a row. Always innovating, Derek is also credited with having conducted the first quiz on Twitter in 2010.

Derek has written over fifty bestselling reference, quiz and textbooks. In 2011, he was voted to the Rajya Sabha as a Member of Parliament (MP) and is the Leader of the Trinamool Congress Parliamentary Party in the Rajya Sabha.

Keep in touch with Derek on Twitter, where his handle is @quizderek.

BUMPER

Quiz Book

DEREK O'BRIEN

RUPA

Published by
Rupa Publications India Pvt. Ltd 2016
7/16, Ansari Road, Daryaganj
New Delhi 110002

Sales Centres:
Allahabad Bengaluru Chennai
Hyderabad Jaipur Kathmandu
Kolkata Mumbai

ISBN: 978-81-291-x x x-x

First impression 2016

10 9 8 7 6 5 4 3 2 1

The moral right of the author has been asserted.

Printed at Shree Maitrey Printech Pvt. Ltd., Noida

HALL OF FAME

**PAST WINNERS OF THE BOURNVITA
QUIZ CONTEST**

1994-1995, Mumbai

Campion High School, Mumbai
Balakrishnan Sivaraman, Sudhanshu Bhuwalka

1995-1996, Mumbai

Kendriya Vidyalaya, Powai, Mumbai
Eipy Koshy, Gourav Shah

1996-1997, Mumbai

Bombay International High School, Mumbai
Nirica Borges, Advait Behara

1997, Mumbai

Mount Saint Mary's School, New Delhi
Joe Christy, Maninder Singh Jessel

1997-1998, Mumbai

Bombay Scottish High School, Mumbai
Shaambhavi Pandyaa, Rahul Lalmalani

1998, Mumbai

Sacred Heart Convent School, Jamshedpur
Ela Verma, Lavanya Raghavan

1998-1999, Mumbai

Indian School Al Ghubra, Muscat
Anand Raghavan, Hitesh Kanvatirtha

1999, Mumbai

Maneckji Cooper High School, Mumbai
Ipsita Bandopadhyay, Gourav Bhattacharya

1999-2000, Mumbai

Chettinad Vidyashram, Chennai
Siddharth, Karthik Das

2000-2001, Mumbai

Bharatiya Vidya Bhavan, Hyderabad
Ananya Bhaskar, Aksha Anand

2001 September, Mumbai

Brightlands, Dehradun
Ankur Bharadwaj, Shray Sharma

2001 December, Mumbai

Little Flower High School, Hyderabad
G. Mithilesh, K Siddharth Reddy

2002 February, Bentota, Sri Lanka

G.D. Birla Centre For Education, Kolkata
Namrata Basu, Rituparna Dey

2002 June, Mumbai

Kerala Samajam Public School, Jamshedpur
Saurav Biswas, Kunal Mohan

2002 September, Mumbai

Jamnabai Narsee School, Mumbai
Sharan Narayanan, Vishnu Shrest

2003 January, Kerala

Naval Public High School, Mumbai
Apoorva Sharma, Abhishek Pandit

2003 May, Kolkata

St. Patrick's Higher Secondary School, Asansol
Pushpen Dasgupta, Shamik Ray

2003 October, Sangla

St. Agnes Loreto Day School, Lucknow
Aastha Srivastava, Illa Gupta

2004 February, Swabhumi, Kolkata

Apeejay School, Jalandhar
Mohit Thukral, Sahil Sareen

2004 May, Goa

Springdales School, Delhi
Anirudh Sridhar, B. Anuraag

2004 July, Indian Military Academy, Dehradun

The Mother's International School, Delhi
Krittika Adhikary, Milind Ganjoo

2004 November, Kolkata

Amity International, New Delhi
Aishwarya Singhal, Adarsh Modi

2005 August, Kolkata
Amity International, New Delhi
Utkarsh Johari/ Aishwarya Singhal

2006 July, Kolkata
Riverdale High School, Dehradun
Kartikeya Panwar/ Sumit Nair

2006 November, Kolkata
Seth Jaipuria School, Lucknow
Ratnaksha Lele/ Ananya Kumar Singh

2011 August, Kolkata
Amity International School, Noida
 Kripi Badonia/ Shinjini Biswas

2012 January, Kolkata
Birla Vidya Niketan, New Delhi
Anusha Malhotra/ Nitya Bansal

2013 January, Kolkata
Vidyaniketan Public School(Ullal), Bengaluru
Shashank Niranjan Gowda, Mainak Mandal

2014 December, Kolkata
Centre Point, Amravati Road, Nagpur
Ratnasambhav Sahu/Tanaya Ramani

SET 1

TAKE YOUR PICK

1. 'Learn from yesterday, live for today, hope for tomorrow. The important thing is not to stop _____.' Fill in the blank to complete this quotation by Albert Einstein.
   a. Wishing
   b. Questioning
   c. Thinking

2. The name of which spice comes from the French word for 'nail'?
   a. Cinnamon
   b. Cardamom
   c. Clove

3. In India, the train Lifeline Express is a...
   a. Hospital
   b. Bank
   c. Primary School

4. Which Asian mountain is also known as the Savage Mountain due to the extreme difficulty of ascent?
   a. Kanchenjunga
   b. K2
   c. Lhotse

5. In 1964, which portfolio was given to Indira Gandhi in the government of Lal Bahadur Shastri?
   a. Defence
   b. Home
   c. Information and Broadcasting

6. In *Alice's Adventures in Wonderland*, which game was played by the Queen of Hearts using hedgehogs as balls?
   a. Quintet
   b. Quidditch
   c. Croquet

7. With which unfortunate incident would you associate the warplane Enola Gay?
   a. Sinking of the ship Bismark
   b. The Hiroshima bombing
   c. Storming of Bastille

8. Odhra Magadha is the precursor to which Indian dance form?
   a. Kuchipudi
   b. Kathak
   c. Odissi

9. Who composed music for the 1969 film *Goopy Gyne Bagha Byne*?
   a. Satyajit Ray
   b. Ravi Shankar
   c. Shiv-Hari

10. Where in the human body is the stapedius muscle situated?
    a. Nose
    b. Ears
    c. Leg

WHAT'S THE QUESTION

1. She lives in St Mary Mead.
2. Kleptomaniac
3. The first batsman to score 10,000 runs in Test cricket.
4. Albumen
5. Ranko the gorilla appeared in this Tintin adventure.
6. It is called a drey.
7. Isohyet
8. Silk Route
9. The Heartbreak Kid
10. Epitaph

MIXED BAG

1. The name of which primate, found only in Madagascar, comes from a Latin word meaning 'spirits of the dead'?
2. Who is the only US president to be awarded the Pulitzer Prize?
3. What does Mysore Paints and Varnishes Limited provide during an election?
4. What is the Pygmallion Point, the extreme southern point of Great Nicobar, now called?
5. Which famous Indian cricketer starred in the 1980

film *Savli Premachi*?

6. Which author's collection of short stories, titled *Soz-e-Watan*, in Urdu was banned by the British?

7. Which is the hardest naturally occurring substance known?

8. Which leader, born in Braunau am Inn, twice failed to secure entry to the Academy of Fine Arts?

9. What is a rockumentary?

10. Tussar, Muga and Endi are varieties of what?

SPOT THE ANSWER

1. What is a pollywog?
    a. A cute golliwog
    b. A green parrot
    c. A tadpole

2. The first session of which of these was held at the Gokuldas Tejpal Sanskrit College?
    a. The Association of Quiz Organizers
    b. The Red Cross in India
    c. The Indian National Congress

3. Sansarpur, often known as the Mecca of Hockey, is located in which state of India?
    a. Punjab
    b. West Bengal
    c. Bihar

4. The construction of which tower started in 1173 AD on a piece of land known as Piazza dei Miracoli?
    a. White House
    b. Eiffel Tower
    c. Leaning Tower of Pisa

5. In the book *The Adventures of Tom Sawyer*, how does the villian, Injun Joe, die?
   a. He is trapped in a cave and dies of starvation.
   b. He drowns in a lake.
   c. A chicken bone gets stuck in his throat.

CONFIDENCE ROUND

1. Which fruit is 'Dussehri' a variety of?
2. How many zeroes are there in 10 crore (100 million)?
3. What do even bald men wear to keep out the sun: caps or cravats?
4. Calcium oxide is another name for quicklime or quicksilver?
5. All leopards have spots: serious or joking?
6. What was Aristotle's nationality?
7. If Juhu beach is in Maharashtra, where is Chowpatty?
8. Which gland swells to a goitre?
9. Who is India's first Formula 1 driver?
10. Which desert fills nearly all of northern Africa?

WHAT'S THE WORD

Set 1

1. Mandolin is a stringed instrument. Serious or Joking?
2. Spaghetti, macaroni and ravioli are varieties of pasta or cheese?
3. In 2004, against which team did Brian Lara score 400 runs in a single Test innings: England or India?
4. Who wrote *The Praise of Folly*: Erasmus or Socrates?

5. Which element forms more compounds than all the other elements combined?
6. Of which small bird are giant, bee and ruby-throated species?
7. What is the word?

Set 2

1. Who is well known for his treatise on geometry called the *Elements*: Euclid or Plato?
2. In Hindu mythology, who was Nakula's mother: Madri or Draupadi?
3. The Louvre Museum is in which capital city: Paris or London?
4. In which country would you be if you land at Baghdad International Airport?
5. Burgundy is dark red or green?
6. What is the strong black coffee, which is made by forcing steam through the ground coffee beans called?
7. What is the word?

Set 3

1. Who was the famous father of Amitabh Bachchan?
2. The name of which continent means 'opposite to the Arctic'?
3. What is the official office of the president of the United States called: Pink House or White House?
4. Which NASA astronaut graduated from Tagore School, Karnal, India, in 1976?
5. *Mammuthus* is the extinct genus of which present-day animal?
6. Which literary character's companion was Friday?

7. What is the word?

Set 4

1. Who played Chandramukhi in Sanjay Leela Bhansali's *Devdas*?
2. In 1985, which team did Sri Lanka defeat to register its first-ever win in ODIs: India or Zimbabwe?
3. What is the capital of Assam?
4. Which word connects a dark brown oval fruit and a number specifying a day?
5. What does 'L' in LASER stand for?
6. Ocular albinism is a genetic condition that primarily affects which organ of the body?
7. What is the word?

Set 5

1. Who was the founder of the Mauryan dynasty: Chandragupta or Brihadratha?
2. Of which fruit are blood, navel and sour varieties: oranges or grapes?
3. In Hindu mythology, Swaha is the wife of which god: Agni or Indra?
4. Vasundhara Raje was the first woman chief minister of which state?
5. With which instrument was Pandit Ravi Shankar associated?
6. Which flightless bird is the second largest living bird?
7. What is the word?

MATHS AND IQ

1. Which number should logically replace the question mark?

   7   49   343   ?

2. Fill in the blanks with either addition, subtraction, multiplication or division to figure out the correct answer. Go sequentially from left to right without following BODMAS.

30		15		4		1	=	5

3. If CRANE=RAN, then SPODE =?

4. Insert the missing number:

   196   (25) 324

   329   ( ) 137

5. Fill in the blanks with either addition, subtraction, multiplication or division to figure out the correct answer. Go sequentially from left to right without following BODMAS.

60		24		14		10	=	7

VOCABULARY

1. Rearrange the letters of the word 'MADE' to get the feminine version of Sir.
2. Rearrange the letters of the word 'LOUSE' to get the name of a Korean city.

3. Rearrange the letters of the word 'MASTER' to get a flowing water body.
4. Read the word 'MART' backwards to get a means of transport.
5. Read the word 'LAID' backwards to get what you do on the telephone.

SPEED

1. What does a Giant Panda's diet mainly consist of?
2. The Statue of Liberty wears a cap, a crown or a garland?
3. How many yolks will one dozen perfect chicken eggs produce?
4. The Simla Agreement of 1972 was signed between India and which other country?
5. Who was the first scientist to describe the laws of motion?
6. Which film maker received an Honorary Oscar for Lifetime Achievement in 1992?
7. Do swimmers float more easily in a swimming pool or in the sea?
8. Which river in Africa means 'Great River' in the language of the Tonga people?
9. Who became the first Indian woman to win an Olympic medal at the 2000 Sydney Olympics?
10. What are the sharp thin leaves of a fir or pine tree called: needles or nails?

ANSWERS

TAKE YOUR PICK

1. Questioning
2. Clove
3. Hospital
4. K2
5. Information and Broadcasting
6. Croquet
7. The Hiroshima bombing
8. Odissi
9. Satyajit Ray
10. Ears

WHAT'S THE QUESTION

1. Where does Miss Marple live?
2. Which word describes a person with a recurrent urge for stealing things?
3. Who is Sunil Gavaskar?
4. What is the white portion of an egg called?
5. What is The Black Island?
6. What do we call a squirrel's nest?
7. What do you call the lines on a map that connect places receiving the same amount of rainfall in a given period?
8. What is the name of the ancient trade route between China and the West?

9. In the World Wrestling Federation, what is Shawn Michaels' nickname?
10. What do you call the words written on a tombstone?

MIXED BAG

1. Lemur
2. John F. Kennedy
3. Indelible ink
4. India Point
5. Sunil Gavaskar
6. Premchand
7. Diamond
8. Adolf Hitler
9. A documentary on rockstars and rock music.
10. Silk

SPOT THE ANSWER

1. A tadpole. The tadpole is the aquatic larval stage of an amphibian.
2. The Indian National Congress. It was founded on 28 December 1885, and played a major role in India's freedom struggle.
3. Punjab
4. Leaning Tower of Pisa
5. He is trapped in a cave and dies of starvation.

CONFIDENCE ROUND

1. Mango

2. Eight
3. Caps
4. Quicklime
5. Serious
6. Greek
7. Also in Maharashtra. Both are located in Mumbai.
8. The thyroid gland
9. Narain Karthikeyan
10. Sahara

WHAT'S THE WORD

Set 1

1. Serious
2. Pasta
3. England
4. Erasmus
5. Carbon
6. Hummingbird
7. SPEECH

Set 2

1. Euclid
2. Madri
3. Paris
4. Iraq
5. Red
6. Espresso
7. EMPIRE

Set 3

1. Harivanshrai Bachchan
2. Antarctica
3. White House
4. Kalpana Chawla
5. Elephant
6. Robinson Crusoe
7. HAWKER

Set 4

1. Madhuri Dixit
2. India
3. Dispur
4. Date
5. Light
6. Eyes
7. MIDDLE

Set 5

1. Chandragupta Maurya
2. Oranges
3. Agni
4. Rajasthan
5. Sitar
6. Emu
7. COARSE

MATHS AND IQ

1. 2401. The consecutive exponents of the digit seven.

2.

30	Divide	15	Plus	4	Minus	1	=	5

3. POD. RAN are the three central letters in the word CRANE, and POD are the central letters in the word SPODE.

4. 25 (Add the digits: $1+9+6+3+2+4=25$, $3+2+9+1+3+7=25$)

5.

60	Plus	24	Minus	14	Divided	10	=	7

VOCABULARY

1. DAME
2. SEOUL
3. STREAM
4. TRAM
5. DIAL

SPEED

1. Bamboo
2. A crown
3. Twelve
4. Pakistan
5. Issac Newton
6. Satyajit Ray
7. In the sea—because of the salt.
8. Zambezi
9. Karnam Malleswari
10. Needles

SET 2

1. Apart from Venus, which planet rotates from east to west?
   a. Jupiter
   b. Mars
   c. Uranus

2. Which country was Herodotus referring to when he said: 'There is no country that possesses so many wonders, nor any, that such a number of works that defy description'?
   a. China
   b. Germany
   c. Egypt

3. Which famous world leader was accused at the Rivonia Trial?
   a. Martin Luther King
   b. Subhas Chandra Bose
   c. Nelson Mandela

4. In Hindu mythology, who has a mansion named Vaijayanta and a sword named Paranjaya?
   a. Vishnu
   b. Shiva
   c. Indra

5. What is parasol a kind of?
   a. Umbrella
   b. Footwear
   c. Bracelet

6. What was the pen name of William Sydney Porter?
   a. Mark Twain
   b. Oscar Wilde
   c. O' Henry

7. Which spice consists of the seed of the Myristica fragrans, a tropical evergreen tree?
   a. Cardamom
   b. Clove
   c. Nutmeg

8. Which leader wrote the *Srimad Bhagavad Gita Rahasya* while he was jailed in Myanmar?
   a. Bal Gangadhar Tilak
   b. Motilal Nehru
   c. Gopal Krishna Gokhale

9. Who was born in Gwalior in 1945 to Haafiz Ali Khan?
   a. Amjad Ali Khan
   b. Bismillah Khan
   c. Ali Akbar Khan

10. Which is the largest internal organ in the human body?
    a. Liver
    b. Heart
    c. Lung

WHAT'S THE QUESTION

1. He is assisted by a group of fellow outlaws known as the 'Merry Men'.
2. Workers, drones and queens
3. Dadamoni
4. Anemometer
5. The first Swede male tennis player to become world number one in the Open era.
6. It is an arrangement of straps placed over an animal's snout.
7. It is a curved piece of wood that can be thrown so that it will return to the thrower.
8. It was built by Gustave Eiffel for the Universal Exposition of 1889, celebrating the centenary of the French Revolution.
9. Boxing Day
10. Jellystone National Park

MIXED BAG

1. Donna Berta di Bernardo left 60 'coins' in her will to Opera Campanilis Petrarum Sancte Marie to buy stones for which tower?
2. Which musician was the music director of the film *Mr & Mrs Iyer*?
3. In *Jack and the Beanstalk*, what was Milky White?
4. In Sikkim, the name of which mountain means 'Five Treasures of the Great Snow'?
5. *Raga Mala* is the autobiography of which famous Indian musician?

6. Why didn't Alexander Graham Bell's mother or his wife use the telephone he invented?
7. How many miles can a full-grown ostrich fly?
8. In terms of the currency notes of India, if MG Series is Mahatma Gandhi Series, what is AP Series?
9. What were originally sold as waist overalls?
10. What is the colour of the Golden Gate Bridge in San Francisco?

SPOT THE ANSWER

1. Who is a cruciverbalist?
   a. An expert at solving crossword puzzles
   b. A person who talks too much
   c. A tightrope walker

2. Kiran Bedi was once a champion in which sport?
   a. Kabaddi
   b. Tennis
   c. Karate

3. Why was the motto 'Be Prepared' chosen for the Boy Scout Movement?
   a. They were Baden-Powell's favourite two words.
   b. For no reason. Just for kicks.
   c. Based on the initials (BP) of its founder

4. How is Princess Manikarnika better known in history?
   a. Steffi Graf (her childhood nickname)
   b. Laika, the first dog in space
   c. Rani Lakshmibai of Jhansi

5. Who resides at 221B, Baker Street?
   a. Dennis the Menace
   b. Popeye
   c. Sherlock Holmes

CONFIDENCE ROUND

1. In 1992, who captained Pakistan to a Cricket World Cup victory?
2. How many days are there in 144 hours?
3. To attain perfect bliss is to attain: nirvana or yoga?
4. Normally, a violin has four, six or eight strings?
5. Which Indian delivered a speech in Chicago in 1893?
6. What means 'mixed bits' in Chinese: chowmein or chop suey?
7. The name of which country starts with 'E' and ends in 'T'?
8. Name the 'park' that John Hammond built on Isla Nublar.
9. The English title of which Salman Khan starrer was *When Love Calls*?
10. In the Ramayana, who was Dasaratha's eldest son?

WHAT'S THE WORD

Set 1

1. Common vampire, winged vampire and hairy-legged vampire are species of which mammal?
2. In literature, which little girl went to Wonderland?
3. What is the chemical symbol of potassium: P or K?
4. Which word announces the end of the first part in a

cinema: interval or interchange?

5. Mount Cook is in New Zealand or Australia?
6. Who was an Italian patriot: Guevara or Garibaldi?
7. What is the word?

Set 2

1. What does 'B' in VIBGYOR stand for: blue or brown?
2. Who saw forty thieves: Ali Baba or Aladdin?
3. Who was married to Raja Gangadhar Rao: Rani Padmini or Rani of Jhansi?
4. Who became chief minister earlier: Sheila Dikshit or Rabri Devi?
5. Which three letters are used as an abbreviation for 'et cetera'?
6. In December 2000, an informal contract was written on a napkin by Charly Rexach to sign which player for FC Barcelona?
7. What is the word?

Set 3

1. The term black panther is generally applied to leopards or lemurs?
2. The name of which part of the human body comes before brow, lash and lid?
3. In which country was Alfred Nobel born?
4. What kind of chips are mostly used in computers: silicon or iron?
5. If 'Z' is the last letter in the English alphabet, then, what is the last letter in the Greek alphabet?
6. Against which team did Sachin Tendulkar score his

only century at the 2003 Cricket World Cup?
7. What is the word?

Set 4

1. All trolleys have wheels: agree or disagree?
2. Who is also known as the Grand Old Man of India: Dadabhai Naoroji or Lala Lajpat Rai?
3. Which state has no coastline: Madhya Pradesh or West Bengal?
4. Who was a character in Shakespeare's *Othello*: Iago or Shylock?
5. What is the state animal of Sikkim?
6. In cricket, under which head are wides, no balls and byes classified?
7. What is the word?

Set 5

1. Copernicus is one of the most prominent craters on the moon: agree or disagree?
2. Who succeeded Jahangir as the Mughal emperor of India?
3. Which word describes a story or film containing events that precede those of an existing work: prequel or sequel?
4. The country Portugal is in which continent?
5. In a leap year, which festival is celebrated on the 360th day of the Gregorian calendar?
6. In a cricket match, what determines which team bats first?
7. What is the word?

MATHS AND IQ

1. Insert the missing number:

24	8
39	13
?	18

2. What should logically replace the question marks?

1	C	5	?
A	3	E	?

3. Fill in the blanks with either addition, subtraction, multiplication or division to figure out the correct answer. Go sequentially from left to right without following BODMAS.

10		30		4		32	=	5

4. Find the odd one out.

    RUGAS

    LEEST

    PORPEC

    NOBREZ

5. Fill in the blanks with either addition, subtraction, multiplication or division to figure out the correct answer. Go sequentially from left to right without following BODMAS.

45		3		10		2	=	7

VOCABULARY

1. Rearrange the letters of the word 'CHAIN' to get the name of a country.
2. Rearrange the letters of the word 'MAUL' (as in

being mauled or eaten by a tiger) to get the name of a white-ish mineral used to purify water or to stop bleeding of cuts.

3. Rearrange the letters of the word 'TABLE' to get the sound a sheep makes.

4. Read the word 'BUS' backwards to get a prefix meaning lower.

5. Read the word 'NOW' backwards to get the basic monetary unit of North and South Korea.

SPEED

1. Which word relating to a geometric figure comes from two Latin words meaning 'around' and 'to carry'?

2. Which metal is alloyed with tin to form bronze?

3. The dance form Kuchipudi originated in West Bengal: serious or joking?

4. The Bhavani Talwar belonged to which famous Indian ruler?

5. A crore is ten million: serious or joking?

6. Which colour forms the background of the flag of the UN?

7. Who is the elder daughter of actress Tanuja?

8. Against which country does Australia play the Border–Gavaskar Test series?

9. What is the Sri Darbar Sahib better known as?

10. Which author's original name was Dhanpat Rai?

ANSWERS

TAKE YOUR PICK

1. Uranus
2. Egypt
3. Nelson Mandela
4. Indra
5. Umbrella
6. O' Henry
7. Nutmeg
8. Bal Gangadhar Tilak
9. Amjad Ali Khan
10. Liver

WHAT'S THE QUESTION

1. Who is Robin Hood?
2. Name three types of honeybees.
3. What was actor Ashok Kumar's nickname?
4. Which instrument is used to measure the speed of wind?
5. Who is Björn Borg?
6. What is a muzzle?
7. What is a boomerang?
8. Why was the Eiffel Tower erected?
9. What is the day after Christmas popularly known as?
10. In which park do Yogi Bear and Boo Boo live?

MIXED BAG

1. Leaning Tower of Pisa
2. Zakir Hussain
3. The name of the cow that Jack traded for some beans.
4. Kanchenjunga
5. Pandit Ravi Shankar
6. They were both deaf.
7. The ostrich cannot fly.
8. Ashokan Pillar Series
9. Jeans
10. Orange

SPOT THE ANSWER

1. An expert at solving crossword puzzles
2. Tennis. She won the Junior Lawn Tennis Championship in 1966, Asian Lawn Tennis Championship in 1972, and the All-India Hard Court Tennis Championship in 1974.
3. Based on the initials (BP) of its founder
4. Rani Lakshmibai of Jhansi
5. Sherlock Holmes

CONFIDENCE ROUND

1. Imran Khan
2. Six
3. Nirvana
4. Four
5. Swami Vivekananda

6. Chop suey
7. Egypt
8. Jurassic Park
9. *Maine Pyar Kiya*
10. Rama

WHAT'S THE WORD

Set 1
1. Bat
2. Alice
3. K
4. Interval
5. New Zealand
6. Garibaldi
7. BAKING

Set 2
1. Blue
2. Ali Baba
3. Rani of Jhansi
4. Rabri Devi
5. Etc.
6. Lionel Messi
7. BARREL

Set 3
1. Leopards
2. Eye
3. Sweden
4. Silicon

5. Omega
6. Namibia
7. LESSON

Set 4

1. Agree
2. Dadabhai Naoroji
3. Madhya Pradesh
4. Iago
5. Red Panda
6. Extras
7. ADMIRE

Set 5

1. Agree
2. Shah Jahan
3. Prequel
4. Europe
5. Christmas
6. Toss
7. ASPECT

MATHS AND IQ

1. 54 (8×3 = 24, 13×3 = 39, so 18×3 = 54)
2. 1   C   5   G
   A   3   E   7
   Every alternate letter starting from A and its numeric position in the alphabet is given.

3. | 10 | Plus | 30 | Multiply | 4 | Divide | 32 | = | 5 |

4. RUGAS (SUGAR). All the others are metals or alloys— STEEL, COPPER, BRONZE.

5.

| 45 | Divide | 3 | Minus | 10 | Plus | 2 | = | 7 |

VOCABULARY

1. CHINA
2. ALUM
3. BLEAT
4. SUB
5. WON

SPEED

1. Circumference
2. Copper
3. Joking. It originated from Andhra Pradesh.
4. Shivaji
5. Serious
6. Blue
7. Kajol
8. India
9. The Golden Temple
10. Munshi Premchand

SET 3

TAKE YOUR PICK

1. After whom is the chemical element with atomic number 102 named?
   a. Albert Einstein
   b. Alfred Bernhard Nobel
   c. Isaac Newton

2. In the Mahabharata, who was granted a divine inward eye so that he could see and relate the events of the battlefield to Dhritarashtra?
   a. Sanjaya
   b. Purochana
   c. Shikhandi

3. The capital of which Scandinavian country is located on the islands of Zealand and Amager?
   a. Norway
   b. Sweden
   c. Denmark

4. Complete this Sunderlal Bahuguna phrase which he coined during the Chipko Movement: 'Ecology is permanent _____.'
   a. Economy
   b. Sociology
   c. Biology

5. By what name is K'ung Fu-tzu better known to the Western world?
   a. Confucius
   b. Lao Tzu
   c. Fa-Hien

6. Which spice was introduced to India around 1800 CE by the East India Company in its spice garden in Courtallam, Tamil Nadu?
   a. Clove
   b. Pepper
   c. Cardamom

7. In *Twenty Thousand Leagues Under the Sea*, what was the name of the warship in which Captain Nemo sailed?
   a. Basillus
   b. Nautilus
   c. Remolus

8. Bidriware derives its name from the town of Bidar. In which state is Bidar located?
   a. Karnataka
   b. Kerala
   c. Gujarat

9. In India, who heads the Department of Space?
   a. The president
   b. The prime minister
   c. The defence minister

10. Which actor won the National Award in the Best Actor category for *Dastak* in 1971 and *Koshish* in 1973?
    a. Dev Anand
    b. Sanjeev Kumar
    c. Dilip Kumar

WHAT'S THE QUESTION

1. It is a piece of paper which indicates that you have paid for something.
2. Hypotenuse
3. A. S. Dileep Kumar (Hint: Music)
4. In the Ramayana, she was Lakshmana and Shatrughna's mother.
5. Aqua regia
6. Duodenum, jejunum and ileum
7. This husk, used to aid digestion, is commercially produced from *P. ovata* and *P. psyllium* in Pakistan and India.
8. This device is a blend of a modulator and a demodulator.
9. Talons
10. This tool is called a jack.

MIXED BAG

1. The motto 'If you desire peace, cultivate justice' is associated with which organisation?
2. In 2001, who became the first Indian girl to be the world junior chess champion?

3. In 1806, which typist's time saver was patented by Ralph Wedgwood?

4. In 1945, who shared the Nobel Prize in medicine with Howard Florey and Ernst Chain?

5. The Russians know this as Kaspiyskoye More. How is it known to us?

6. Which character by Charles Dickens is famous for his request: 'Please sir, may I have some more'?

7. What are brood parasites?

8. The twenty-five windows in which monument symbolise the gemstones found on Earth?

9. What food makes the cartoon character Popeye strong?

10. Which famous Kushan ruler was referred to as Chia-ni-se-chia in Chinese?

SPOT THE ANSWER

1. Why did the British settle in houseboats in Kashmir?
   a. They were barred from buying land to convert into resorts
   b. To protect their daughters from mixing with 'locals'
   c. The city was too congested and dirty

2. In 1906, which word was first coined by Maganlal Gandhi in the South African journal *Indian Opinion*?
   a. Ahimsa
   b. Satyagraha
   c. Harijan

3. In Japan, who was called 'Maikeru Jakuson'?
   a. The eldest son of the emperor
   b. Michael Jackson
   c. Eldest daughter of the emperor

4. How did the Hope diamond get its name?
   a. It is named after Henry Philip Hope who owned it in the 1830s
   b. It is named by the person who first mined it
   c. It is named after the Hope River in New Zealand

5. Carl Lewis does not have his 100 metre gold medal from the 1984 Olympics. Why?
   a. He lost it while swimming in the Niagara Falls.
   b. He donated it to UNICEF.
   c. He put it in his father's coffin.

CONFIDENCE ROUND

1. Kalidas wrote in Sanskrit or Tamil?
2. The presence of which element makes the blood red: iron or copper?
3. According to legend, which instrument did Nero play while Rome burnt?
4. Salt is used to preserve food: serious or joking?
5. The Solang Valley is in Himachal Pradesh or Arunachal Pradesh?
6. A cycling competition is usually held in: an aerodrome or a velodrome?
7. If you used your hand to play a 'harmonium', what would you use to play a 'harmonica'?

8. Which Nobel Prize winner was a teacher at St Mary's High School, Kolkata, from 1931 to 1948?
9. Which film director was awarded the Bharat Ratna in 1992?
10. Which mythical ruler had the 'golden touch'?

WHAT'S THE WORD

Set 1

1. Which is a shade of purple: tan or mauve?
2. Which king adopted the policy of 'conquest by dharma': Samudragupta or Ashoka?
3. The cricket team of which country has been named after its national flower, proteas?
4. In Greece, what is 'feta' a type of: cheese or butter?
5. The stripes of which animal are sometimes called 'follow me' stripes helping the young ones follow their mothers through the forest: giraffe or okapi?
6. Which set of cards, used in fortune telling, is divided into two groups called Major Arcana and Minor Arcana?
7. What is the word?

Set 2

1. With which sport is a 'dohyo' associated: sumo or judo?
2. Which of these is a snake-like fish: an eel or a seal?
3. Which ornament is worn around the neck: a bracelet or a choker?
4. In the official name of India, what comes before India: Republic or Union?

5. The River Volga flows through which continent?
6. Which Hindi film actress' sister is Farah Naaz?
7. What is the word?

Set 3

1. Which Indian prime minister was the son of another Indian prime minister?
2. In the country UAE, what does 'E' stand for: Empire or Emirates?
3. In Pakistan, what is a rupee divided into: paisa or cent?
4. How many arms does an octopus have?
5. *The Night Watch* was one of which painter's most well-known paintings?
6. What is the costume of a female ballet dancer called: Tutu or Tunic?
7. What is the word?

Set 4

1. Which game gets its name from the public school in Warwickshire, England, where it was first played: Rugby or Cricket?
2. Harry Potter could talk to snakes: agree or disagree?
3. In the abbreviation NATO, what does 'N' stand for?
4. Which capital city of India is also known as the 'adobe of Drona'?
5. The name of which fruit comes from the Arabic word *naranj*?
6. Which Dessau-born scholar was the son of the Romantic poet Wilhelm Müller?
7. What is the word?

Set 5

1. Which religious leader died at Kushinagar: Buddha or Mahavira?
2. What is the hard covering of the crown of teeth called: enamel or canine?
3. The characters Sheriff Woody, Buzz Lightyear and Mr Potato Head appear in which animated film series?
4. What is the name of the cylindrical clay oven in which naans are made: tandoor or kadhai?
5. In which country is the Aswan High Dam located?
6. Which of these was the first man-made fibre: Rayon or Rubber?
7. What is the word?

MATHS AND IQ

1. An anagram of this author's name is, very aptly, 'I'll make a wise phrase'. Who is he?
2. An express train leaves Kolkata for Mumbai at the same time as a passenger train leaves Mumbai for Kolkata. Which is farther from Kolkata when they meet? (Express train average speed: 60 km/hr; Passenger train average speed: 30 km/hr)
3. Fill in the blanks with either addition, subtraction, multiplication or division to figure out the correct answer. Go sequentially from left to right without following BODMAS.

15		4		7		62	=	5

4. 100 cats killed 100 rats in three minutes. How many minutes did three cats take to kill three rats?

5. Fill in the blanks with either addition, subtraction, multiplication or division to figure out the correct answer. Go sequentially from left to right without following BODMAS.

85		36		7		1	=	7

VOCABULARY

1. Rearrange the letters of the word 'DAWN' to get what magicians sometimes use.
2. Rearrange the letters of the word 'CLAM' to get a word meaning serene.
3. Rearrange the letters of the word 'SHORE' to get an animal.
4. Read the word 'KEEP' backwards to get a four-letter word meaning to take a brief look at something.
5. Read the word 'DEED' backwards to get a word that means 'an act or action'.

SPEED

1. Which great Indian leader's surname sounds like a religious mark on the forehead?
2. Who played the role of Itzhak Stern in the 1993 film *Schindler's List*?
3. Spider, hermit and horseshoe are varieties of which creature?
4. The India Gate is in Mumbai: serious or joking?
5. In India, which sport is played in Durand Cup?
6. What is informally called a chopper: a tram or a helicopter?

7. Who was the first prime minister of India to receive the Bharat Ratna?
8. What carries blood away from the heart?
9. What is measured on a spring balance?
10. From which famous town did the Pied Piper take away all the children?

ANSWERS

TAKE YOUR PICK

1. Alfred Bernhard Nobel
2. Sanjaya
3. Denmark
4. Economy
5. Confucius
6. Clove
7. Nautilus
8. Karnataka
9. The prime minister
10. Sanjeev Kumar

WHAT'S THE QUESTION

1. What is a receipt?
2. In a right-angled triangle, what do you call the side opposite the right angle?
3. What is music composer A. R. Rahman's real name?
4. In the Ramayana, who was Sumitra?
5. What is the popular name for a mixture of concentrated nitric and hydrochloric acids, used for dissolving gold?
6. Name the three parts of the small intestine.
7. What is isabgol?
8. What is a modem?
9. What are a bird of prey's hooked claws called?

10. What tool is used to raise a car when a tyre needs changing?

MIXED BAG

1. ILO (International Labour Organization)
2. Koneru Humpy
3. Carbon paper
4. Alexander Fleming
5. Caspian Sea
6. Oliver Twist
7. Birds that lay their eggs in other birds' nests and have the foster parents take care of them, e.g. cuckoo.
8. The Statue of Liberty
9. Spinach
10. Kanishka

SPOT THE ANSWER

1. They were barred from buying land to convert into resorts
2. Satyagraha
3. Michael Jackson (Maikeru is Japanese for Michael)
4. It is named after Henry Philip Hope who owned it in the 1830s
5. He put it in his father's coffin

CONFIDENCE ROUND

1. Sanskrit
2. Iron

3. The fiddle
4. Serious
5. Himachal Pradesh
6. Velodrome
7. Hands and lips
8. Mother Teresa
9. Satyajit Ray
10. Midas

WHAT'S THE WORD

Set 1

1. Mauve
2. Ashoka
3. South Africans
4. Cheese
5. Okapi
6. Tarot cards
7. MASCOT

Set 2

1. Sumo
2. Eel
3. Choker
4. Republic
5. Europe
6. Tabu
7. SECRET

Set 3

1. Rajiv Gandhi

2. Emirates
3. Paisa
4. Eight
5. Rembrandt
6. Tutu
7. REPORT

Set 4

1. Rugby
2. Agree
3. North
4. Dehradun
5. Orange
6. Max Müller
7. RANDOM

Set 5

1. Buddha
2. Enamel
3. The *Toy Story* series
4. Tandoor
5. Egypt
6. Rayon
7. BETTER

MATHS AND IQ

1. William Shakespeare
2. Neither. When they meet they will be the same distance from Kolkata.
3.

| 15 | Multiply | 4 | Plus | 7 | Minus | 62 | = | 5 |

4. Three minutes

5.

| 85 | Minus | 36 | Divide | 7 | Multiply | 1 | = | 7 |

VOCABULARY

1. WAND
2. CALM
3. HORSE
4. PEEK
5. DEED

SPEED

1. Bal Gangadhar Tilak
2. Ben Kingsley
3. Crabs
4. Joking; it is in New Delhi
5. Football
6. Helicopter
7. Jawaharlal Nehru
8. The arteries
9. Weight
10. Hamelin

SET 4

TAKE YOUR PICK

1. Adams, Leverrier, Galle and Lassell are some of the rings of which planet?
   a. Neptune
   b. Saturn
   c. Jupiter
2. In the Mahabharata, who among these was killed by Krishna?
   a. Karna
   b. Ekalavya
   c. Jayadratha
3. Which famous philosopher was also the tutor of Alexander the Great?
   a. Aristotle
   b. Socrates
   c. Rousseau
4. What was defined as 'three grains of barley, dry and round, placed end to end lengthwise'?
   a. Centimetre
   b. Millimetre
   c. Inch
5. The name of which of these means the 'gilded one' in Spanish?
   a. El Dorado

b. Buenos Aires

c. El Nino

6. Which 1852 book was smuggled into Russia in Yiddish to evade the czarist censor?

a. *Uncle Tom's Cabin*

b. *Alice in Wonderland*

c. *Das Kapital*

7. Who was the prime minister of the United Kingdom at the time of Queen Elizabeth II's coronation?

a. Neville Chamberlain

b. Winston Churchill

c. Harold McMillan

8. Tomato, sweet corn, oxtail, bird's nest, chimney and French onion are all …

a. Types of soup

b. Breeds of cats

c. Sporting events

9. Which work is often referred to as the fifth veda?

a. *Panchtantra*

b. *Natyashastra*

c. *Arthshastra*

10. Which Indi-pop singer was born Sujata, and was known for her hit 'Made in India'?

a. Sunita Rao

b. Alisha Chinai

c. Pravati Khan

WHAT'S THE QUESTION

1. In *Winnie the Pooh*, she is Roo's mother.

2. He directed the film *Kuch Kuch Hota Hai*.
3. Harmattan
4. Varicella
5. The author of *A House for Mr Biswas*
6. In Western astrology, it is the second sign of the zodiac.
7. Mezzanine
8. Howard Carter
9. This country was once known as South West Africa.
10. Hydrophobia is its other name.

MIXED BAG

1. Why were copper rivets put on denim jeans?
2. The name of which country, situated partly in Europe and partly in Asia, is also the name of a bird?
3. Which scientist was offered the presidency of Israel after Chaim Weizmann's death in 1952?
4. During the construction of which monument was a small town called Mumtazabad built for the workers?
5. Which famous novel begins with the words 'Call me Ishmael'?
6. My father won a Padma Bhushan in 1976, my wife won a Padma Shri in 1992 and I have received a Padma Shri, a Padma Bhushan and a Padma Vibhushan. Who am I?
7. In *Tintin* comics, who is called Milou in French?
8. Which popular song during the War of American Independence is the republic's unofficial national anthem?
9. The north Indian drink *kanji* is normally made with

a vegetable whose scientific name is *Daucus carota sativis*. How is this vegetable better known?
10. Which cricketer played the role of a villain in the film *Kabhi Ajnabi The*?

SPOT THE ANSWER

1. For what was a Kashmiri natural dye called 'rattanjog' previously used?
   a. To dye the shawl pashmina
   b. To give the dish roganjosh its red colour
   c. It was mixed with mehendi for dyeing hair

2. What does an ichthyologist study?
   a. The cause of itch and other skin diseases
   b. Fish
   c. Comics

3. What is a croissant?
   a. A crescent-shaped (bread-like) roll made of yeast
   b. A cross-stitch in embroidery
   c. An African spider

4. Who is a shoeblack?
   a. He removes the make-up of actresses.
   b The correct term for a person who polishes shoes for a living.
   c. He looks after the slippers/shoes of coal miners.

5. Which present-day city was established by Dost Mohammed Khan in 1724?

    a. Bhopal
    b. Kanpur
    c. Udaipur

CONFIDENCE ROUND

1. Who was the first Indian to win the Miss Universe title?
2. Who is the first Indian prime minister to hold office for more than one term?
3. If you aren't careful, in which of these games can you go bankrupt: Ludo or Monopoly?
4. Which is longer: the small or the large intestine?
5. S.D. Burman composed the music for *Sholay*: serious or joking?
6. Which capital city was formerly called Pataligram and Kusumpur?
7. Which is the longest of the five tributaries of the Indus river?
8. Who was the author of *Hitopadesha*?
9. In India, how many digits comprise the PNR number on a railway ticket?
10. Which world famous magician shares his name with the title character of a Charles Dickens novel?

WHAT'S THE WORD

Set 1

1. Where does tartar accumulate: teeth or toes?
2. Who was older: Ashok Kumar or Kishore Kumar?
3. What is a religious teacher of the Jewish community

called: a rabbi or a synagogue?

4. Who became the secretary of the Ahmedabad Textile Labour Association in 1992: Gulzarilal Nanda or Indira Gandhi?
5. What number batsman comes to bat after the sixth wicket falls?
6. Which state is famous for Tanjore paintings?
7. What is the word?

Set 2

1. Which country has a tricolour flag with white, blue and red bands: Canada or Russia?
2. What name is commonly given to the code of polite behaviour in society: epithet or etiquette?
3. Which surname is shared by the man who discovered Tutankhamun's tomb and the thirty-ninth US president: Carter or Clinton?
4. Biju Patnaik and his son Naveen Patnaik have been chief ministers of which Indian state?
5. In human blood, cells of which colour carry haemoglobin?
6. Commonly, which seven-letter name is given to a microcomputer suitable for use at an ordinary desk?
7. What is the word?

Set 3

1. Which of these is usually not encased in a shell: a walnut or a raisin?
2. What are most reptiles classified as: ectothermic or endothermic?
3. Dr John Watson is the companion of which fictional

character?

4. In India, what does 'I' in CBI stand for: investigation or intelligence?
5. Which five-letter word meaning 'magnificent' comes before Canyon and Slam?
6. Who was the famous mother of Sanjay Dutt?
7. What is the word?

Set 4

1. A parakeet is a seed eating parrot or woodpecker?
2. Which actress acted in Gurinder Chadha's *Bride and Prejudice*: Sushmita Sen or Aishwarya Rai?
3. Which fairy-tale character is famous for her long hair: Cinderella or Rapunzel?
4. In which Indian state is the annual Pushkar Fair held: Haryana or Rajasthan?
5. Which month gets its name from the Latin word for 'eight'?
6. Which cuddly toy was invented in honour of Theodore Roosevelt?
7. What is the word?

Set 5

1. What are bristol and bond two grades of: cheese or paper?
2. Grapes can also be black in colour: agree or disagree?
3. Which capital do Punjab and Haryana share: Srinagar or Chandigarh?
4. Which temperature scale is named after the British physicist William Thomson?
5. Which word is used to describe two objects or places at equal distances?

6. In computers, what is a program designed to breach security in the guise of performing some harmless function called?

7. What is the word?

MATHS AND IQ

1. Which is the odd one out and why?
   NEALPT, BRIBTA, XLAGYA, MCEOT

2. Fill in the blanks with either addition, subtraction, multiplication or division to figure out the correct answer. Go sequentially from left to right without following BODMAS.

25		5		55		7	=	10

3. Insert the word that completes the first word and starts the next. (Clue: Animal) C (...) X

4. If DRIVER = 7 PEDESTRIAN = 11 Then, ACCIDENT =?

5. Fill in the blanks with either addition, subtraction, multiplication or division to figure out the correct answer. Go sequentially from left to right without following BODMAS.

36		2		24		8	=	12

VOCABULARY

1. Rearrange the letters of the word 'NOSE' to get the name of a river in Bihar.

2. Rearrange the letters of the word 'RAP' to get a golfing term.

3. Rearrange the letters of the word 'WHAT' to get a

word to describe the melting of snow.

4. Read the word 'REWARD' backwards to find a compartment in your desk.
5. Read the word 'RATS' backwards to find a heavenly body.

SPEED

1. In the nursery rhyme *Hey Diddle Diddle*, who ran away with the spoon?
2. A meteorologist studies meteors: serious or joking?
3. Which country did Moses lead his people out of?
4. Which is not a martial art: kung fu, ikebana or judo?
5. Which continent has half the world's population?
6. Snoopy and Charlie Brown appear in which comic strip, which has an edible name?
7. Only female *Anopheles* mosquitoes can transmit malaria or dengue?
8. What was the most common colour of tennis balls before yellow was introduced?
9. Louis Braille was born blind: serious or joking?
10. From where did Shivaji escape by hiding inside a basket: Lucknow or Agra?

ANSWERS

TAKE YOUR PICK

1. Neptune
2. Ekalavya
3. Aristotle
4. Inch
5. El Dorado
6. *Uncle Tom's Cabin*
7. Winston Churchill
8. Types of soup
9. *Natyashastra*
10. Alisha Chinai

WHAT'S THE QUESTION

1. Who is Kanga?
2. Who is Karan Johar?
3. What is the name of a well-known West African trade wind?
4. What is the medical term for chicken pox?
5. Who is V.S. Naipaul?
6. What is Taurus?
7. What do you call the storey of a building which is between the two main floors?
8. Name the British archaeologist who discovered the largely intact tomb of King Tutankhamen.
9. By what name was Namibia formerly known?

10. By what other name is rabies known?

MIXED BAG

1. To prevent the pockets from tearing under the weight of tools and to increase their durability.
2. Turkey
3. Albert Einstein
4. Taj Mahal
5. *Moby Dick*
6. Amitabh Bachchan
7. Snowy
8. Yankee Doodle
9. Carrot
10. Syed Kirmani (It also featured cricketer Sandip Patil.)

SPOT THE ANSWER

1. To give the dish *roganjosh* its red colour
2. Fish
3. A crescent-shaped (bread-like) roll made of yeast
4. The correct term for a person who polishes shoes for a living
5. Bhopal

CONFIDENCE ROUND

1. Sushmita Sen
2. Jawaharlal Nehru
3. Monopoly
4. Small intestine

5. Joking. The music was composed by his son R.D. Burman.
6. Patna
7. Sutlej
8. Narayana Pandit
9. Ten
10. David Copperfield

WHAT'S THE WORD

Set 1

1. Teeth
2. Ashok Kumar
3. Rabbi
4. Gulzari Lal Nanda
5. Eight
6. Tamil Nadu
7. TARGET

Set 2

1. Russia
2. Etiquette
3. Carter; Howard Carter and Jimmy Carter
4. Odisha
5. Red
6. Desktop
7. RECORD

Set 3

1. Raisin
2. Ectothermic

3. Sherlock Holmes
4. Investigation
5. Grand
6. Nargis
7. RESIGN

Set 4

1. Parrot
2. Aishwarya Rai
3. Rapunzel
4. Rajasthan
5. October
6. Teddy bear
7. PARROT

Set 5

1. Paper
2. Agree
3. Chandigarh
4. Kelvin scale
5. Equidistant
6. Trojan Horse
7. PACKET

MATHS AND IQ

1. BRIBTA (RABBIT—an animal). The others are associated with space—COMET, GALAXY, PLANET.

2.
| 25 | Multiply | 5 | Minus | 55 | Divided | 7 | = | 10 |

3. APE

4. 9 (DRIVER has 6 letters +1 = 7, PEDESTRIAN has 10 letters + 1=11, ACCIDENT has 8 letters+1=9)

5.

36	Multiply	2	Plus	24	Divided	8	=	12

VOCABULARY

1. SONE
2. PAR
3. THAW
4. DRAWER
5. STAR

SPEED

1. The dish
2. Joking; he studies the atmosphere and weather
3. Egypt
4. Ikebana
5. Asia
6. *Peanuts*
7. Malaria
8. White
9. Joking; he lost his vision by the age of three
10. Agra

SET 5

1. Which of these elements is not named after a scientist?
   a. Einsteinium
   b. Ruthenium
   c. Curium

2. In which present-day country was the Battle of Waterloo fought?
   a. France
   b. Iran
   c. Belgium

3. Which rakshasa took the form of a golden deer to lure Lakshmana away, leaving Sita unprotected?
   a. Tadaka
   b. Mareecha
   c. Nikumbha

4. In India, 'Duty Unto Death' is the motto of which organization?
   a. Border Security Force
   b. National Cadet Corps
   c. Central Bureau of Investigation

5. Which country's highest peak is Mount Ararat?
   a. China
   b. Turkey
   c. Iran

6. What do you call a system of serving when a meal, consisting of several dishes is set out and guests serve themselves?
   a. Buffet
   b. A la carte
   c. Menu

7. With which artist would you associate *The Thinker*, a statue cast in bronze?
   a. Auguste Rodin
   b. Michelangelo
   c. Leonardo da Vinci

8. Kisan Ghat in Delhi is the memorial ground of which famous leader?
   a. Charan Singh
   b. Rajiv Gandhi
   c. Jagjivan Ram

9. Edward Lear was famous for his five-line humorous poems. What is the correct term for this style of poetry?
   a. Elegy
   b. Sonnet
   c. Limerick

10. Which character did actor Leonard Nimoy portray in *Star Trek V: The Final Frontier*?
    a. Spock
    b. Kirk
    c. McCoy

WHAT'S THE QUESTION

1. This is where leather is produced from animal skins.
2. It was the last capital of the kingdom of Vijayanagar.
3. Collage
4. In a 1982 film, he came to Earth and wanted to call home.
5. The SI unit of energy or work is named after this scientist.
6. Anastasia and Drizella (Hint: Children's literature)
7. This J-shaped elastic sac is the widest part of the digestive system.
8. In comics, Lothar is his best friend and crime-fighting companion.
9. Hellas
10. Chandigarh was planned by this French architect.

MIXED BAG

1. Which river is the largest drainage system in the world in terms of the volume of its flow and the area of its basin?
2. Issued by Sweden, what kind of an object is the Treskilling Yellow?
3. Whose most well-known poems are contained in the

collection *Barrack-Room Ballads*?

4. In 1961, which Indian state was liberated from Portuguese rule?
5. In which state of India is the only floating national park in the world located?
6. Ivan Lendl and Martina Navratilova represented USA in international competitions later in their careers. Which country did they originally belong to by birth?
7. Whose sacred tooth is said to be at Sri Lanka's Temple of the Tooth?
8. Supremo, a famous comic-strip character of the 1980s, was styled after which Hindi film actor?
9. With which Indian community would you associate the dal-meat preparation called 'dhansak'?
10. The word 'hygiene' is named after the Greek goddess of what?

SPOT THE ANSWER

1. If you were staying at 'The Y', where would you be staying?
   a. The YMCA
   b. The headquarters of Mahesh Yogi
   c. Yamini Krishnamurthy's Dance Academy

2. How did Mount Everest get its name?
   a. After Sir George Everest, the then Surveyor General of India
   b. After the Greek god of mountains
   c. Edmund Hillary's childhood nickname was 'Everest'

3. Who among these is most likely to use a gavel?
    a. Pilot
    b. Judge
    c. Puppeteer

4. What did Pingali Venkaiah design, which was adopted by India's Constituent Assembly on 22 July 1947?
    a. The Indian National Flag
    b. Madhuri Dixit's costumes in Khalnayak
    c. The Rashtrapati Bhavan

5. On what grounds was Surendranath Banerjee's admission to the Indian Civil Service (now IAS) rejected?
    a. He misrepresented his age
    b. His IQ was below fifty-five
    c. Because only women were allowed in the ICS

CONFIDENCE ROUND

1. Which four-letter word is used to describe the male protagonist of a film?
2. Who was the first woman to win the Nobel Prize?
3. Which animal has been on the logo of WWF since 1961?
4. Which country is known for its dykes: Holland or Spain?
5. Which character was created by Charles Dickens: Oliver Twist or Tom Brown?
6. The local name of the Indian wild dog sounds like which percussion instrument?
7. Which London-based football club has been coached

by Arsene Wenger?

8. Which cookery show host wrote *Khazana of Indian Vegetarian Recipes*?

9. Pakistan has a larger population than Russia: serious or joking?

10. Who had a horse named Bucephalus?

WHAT'S THE WORD

Set 1

1. Which steel city lies along the Damodar river: Bokaro or Bilaspur?

2. Which of these is the largest living bird: ostrich or rhea?

3. Most skyscrapers are vertical or horizontal?

4. Which superhero was born in Long Island, New York, to Howard Anthony Stark and Maria Collins Carbonell Stark?

5. During which festival are snakes worshipped: Nag Panchami or Raksha Bandhan?

6. How many unit lengths will you use moving from minus 1 to 7?

7. What is the word?

Set 2

1. Which of these are more in number: countries or continents?

2. Which of these is the capital of Peru: Santiago or Lima?

3. What is a dome-shaped Eskimo house, typically built from blocks of solid snow, called?

4. Kim Jong-il was a leader of which country: South

Korea or North Korea?

5. Give me a four-letter word for 'a soft, white substance formed when milk sours, used as the basis for cheese'.

6. Which of these parts of the human body serves as a pump: kidney or heart?

7. What is the word?

Set 3

1. What are bowler and sombrero types of?

2. Which river is called *Nahr al Furat* in Arabic: Jordan or Euphrates?

3. In which city is the Lord's cricket ground located: Manchester or London?

4. Which rock constitutes an estimated 95 per cent of the upper part of the Earth's crust: igneous or sedimentary?

5. Which scheduled language of India is an official language of Pakistan?

6. According to the proverb, what does a rolling stone not gather?

7. What is the word?

Set 4

1. Ra is the chemical symbol of which element?

2. Which of these organisations has France and Belgium as its members: European Union or OPEC (Organization of Petroleum Exporting Countries)?

3. Ants can lift and carry more than three times their own weight: serious or joking?

4. Which Indian prime minister was born on 4 December

1919, in Jhelum?

5. In Hindu mythology, who was Lakshmana's father?
6. Conjunctiva is a part of which organ of the human body?
7. What is the word?

Set 5

1. In which language was the Ramayana originally composed: Hindi or Sanskrit?
2. Which district is in the state of Uttar Pradesh: Etah or Bellary?
3. Which nut is shaped like a bean: chestnut or cashew nut?
4. What is also known as lockjaw: tetanus or conjunctivitis?
5. The scientific name of which bird is *Struthio camelus*?
6. Which flower is the symbol of the British Labour Party?
7. What is the word?

MATHS AND IQ

1. Find the number that logically completes the series: 2, 3, 5, 9, 17, _____
2. Use the digit '4' four times and the bracket, addition, subtraction, multiplication or division symbols to make the digit 3.
3. Fill in the blanks with either addition, subtraction, multiplication or division to figure out the correct answer. Go sequentially from left to right without following BODMAS.

54		34		10		5	=	10

4. A zookeeper was asked to count the number of birds and animals in a zoo. He counted thirty heads and a hundred feet. Find the number of birds and the number of animals in the zoo.

5. Fill in the blanks with either addition, subtraction, multiplication or division to figure out the correct answer. Go sequentially from left to right without following BODMAS.

33		11		43		34	=	12

VOCABULARY

1. Rearrange the letters of the word 'SPICE' to describe books like the Ramayana and Mahabharata.
2. Rearrange the letters of the word 'PETAL' to find something on the dining table.
3. Rearrange the letters of the word 'RESIST' to get a member of your family.
4. Read the word 'GUM' backwards to get a drinking vessel.
5. Read the word 'TIDE' backwards to get a word that means to prepare for publication by correcting or modifying written material.

SPEED

1. What do you call the result of multiplying two numbers?
2. Who was born earlier: Albert Einstein or Isaac Newton?

3. When you add a post-script to a letter, which two letters of the alphabet do you use?
4. Mount Godwin Austen is also known as M2 or K2?
5. Which colour is used to describe cinema tickets bought illegally?
6. In which country was Sir Donald Bradman born?
7. Which famous Dickens character's stepfather was Mr Edward Murdstone?
8. Flying foxes are bats: serious or joking?
9. Where would you find your palm: hand or leg?
10. Bahadur Shah II was the last ruler of which dynasty?

ANSWERS

TAKE YOUR PICK

1. Ruthenium. Ruthenium is named after a region of central Europe, Curium is named after the Curies, Einsteinium is named after Einstein.
2. Belgium
3. Mareecha
4. Border Security Force
5. Turkey (Greater Ararat)
6. Buffet
7. Auguste Rodin
8. Charan Singh
9. Limerick
10. Spock

WHAT'S THE QUESTION

1. What is a tannery?
2. What is Hampi?
3. What do you call a piece of art made by sticking different materials such as photographs and pieces of paper or fabric on to a surface?
4. Who was the lovable alien ET?
5. Who was James Prescott Joule?
6. Who were Cinderella's stepsisters?
7. What is the stomach?
8. Who is Mandrake?

9. What is the Greek name for Greece and appears on its stamps?
10. Who was Le Corbusier?

MIXED BAG

1. Amazon
2. Stamp
3. Rudyard Kipling
4. Goa
5. Manipur. Keibul Lamjao National Park
6. Czechoslovakia
7. Gautama Buddha
8. Amitabh Bachchan
9. Parsis
10. Health

SPOT THE ANSWER

1. The YMCA. The Young Men's Christian Association is a world-wide Christian voluntary movement for women and men, seeking to build a community based on love, peace and reconciliation.
2. After Sir George Everest, the then Surveyor General of India. Sir George Everest was the Surveyor General of India in 1830–1843. He is credited with completing the trigonometric survey of India. Mount Everest was renamed in his honour, from Peak XV, in 1865.
3. Judge
4. The Indian National Flag
5. He misrepresented his age

CONFIDENCE ROUND

1. Hero
2. Marie Curie
3. Giant panda
4. Holland; dykes are embankments built to prevent flooding from the sea.
5. Oliver Twist
6. Dhol. The name of the dog is Dhole.
7. Arsenal
8. Sanjeev Kapoor
9. Serious; Pakistan's population is 196,174,380 (est) while Russia's is 142,470,272 (est).
10. Alexander

WHAT'S THE WORD

Set 1

1. Bokaro
2. Ostrich
3. Vertical
4. Iron Man
5. Nag Panchami
6. Eight
7. BOVINE

Set 2

1. Countries
2. Lima
3. Igloo
4. North Korea

5. Curd
6. Heart
7. CLINCH

Set 3

1. Hats
2. Euphrates
3. London
4. Igneous
5. Urdu
6. Moss
7. HELIUM

Set 4

1. Radium
2. European Union
3. Serious
4. I.K. Gujral
5. Dasharatha
6. Eye
7. RESIDE

Set 5

1. Sanskrit
2. Etah
3. Cashew nut
4. Tetanus
5. Ostrich
6. Rose
7. SECTOR

MATHS AND IQ

1. 33 (2+1=3, 3+2=5, 5+4=9, 9+8=17, 17+16=33)
2. 3= (4+4+4)/4
3.

54	Minus	34	Divided	10	Multiply	5	=	10

4. Birds=10, Animals=20
5.

33	Divide	11	Plus	43	Minus	34	=	12

VOCABULARY

1. EPICS
2. PLATE
3. SISTER
4. MUG
5. EDIT

SPEED

1. The product
2. Isaac Newton
3. P.S.
4. K2
5. Black
6. Australia
7. David Copperfield
8. Serious
9. Hand
10. Mughal

SET 6

TAKE YOUR PICK

1. Collectively, how many moons do the planets Mercury and Venus have?
    a. One
    b. None
    c. Fifty-five

2. The Chinese pilgrim Fa-hien visited Kannauj between 399 and 414 A. D. during the reign of…
    a. Chandragupta II
    b. Ashoka
    c. Kanishka

3. Which deity is credited with teaching Ayurveda to Sushruta?
    a. Vishwakarma
    b. Dhanwantari
    c. Charaka

4. In which device might you come across a trackball?
    a. TV camera
    b. Computer
    c. Watch

5. What island did Peter Minuit acquire for sixty guilders from the Native Americans?

    a. Manhattan Island
    b. Christmas Island
    c. Galapagos Island

6. Which of these herbs, used extensively in Indian cuisine, is referred to as *dhania* in Hindi?
    a. Coriander
    b. Fenugreek
    c. Asafoetida

7. Sir Winston Churchill visited which country during its years under British rule and called it 'the pearl of Africa'?
    a. Somalia
    b. Uganda
    c. South Africa

8. Jatra is a traditional theatre form of which state of India?
    a. Andhra Pradesh
    b. West Bengal
    c. Maharashtra

9. Abraham Ortelius's book, *Theatrum Orbis Terrarum*, which means 'Theatre of the World', is generally believed to be the first modern example of what?
    a. Atlas
    b. Dictionary
    c. Encyclopedia

10. Which of these Raj Kapoor starrers was also released

as *The Vagabond*?
a. *Barsaat*
b. *Awara*
c. *Shri 420*

WHAT'S THE QUESTION

1. In Roman numerals it is expressed as MXC.
2. This Mughal emperor was born in Fergana in 1483.
3. Pedicure
4. In the Mahabharata, she was the only sister of Duryodhana.
5. Victor, Laverne and Hugo
6. The lady in this painting is thought to be Lisa Gherardini.
7. Khyber Pass
8. In 1962, John Glenn Jr was the first man to do this.
9. Shatabdi Express was flagged off in 1988 to commemorate his 100th birth anniversary.
10. Alopecia is the medical term.

MIXED BAG

1. Lord Krishna was born when Vishnu sent a black hair into Devaki's womb. Who was born when he sent a white hair into Rohini's womb?
2. The region of Macau, which was a colony of Portugal till 1999 is now part of which country?
3. In India, which leader's death anniversary is celebrated as Anti-Terrorism Day?
4. In the *Secret Seven* books, what is the name of Peter

and Janet's golden spaniel?

5. In 1661, which Indian city was given to King Charles II as part of the dowry when he married Princess Catherine de Braganza of Portugal?

6. Which fruit is also known as Chinese gooseberry?

7. Nadia Comaneci was the first woman to obtain a perfect 10 in Olympic gymnastics. Who was the first man?

8. What did Gutzon Borglum and his son Lincoln leave behind in the Black Hills of South Dakota, USA?

9. I was popularly known as M.S. I was born in Madurai. I received the Bharat Ratna in 1998. Who am I?

10. Which film by Satyajit Ray was completed when Dr B.C. Roy, former chief minister of West Bengal, provided funds from the Public Works Department, on the grounds that 'path' was a matter within the PWD's jurisdiction?

SPOT THE ANSWER

1. Why was champion swimmer Dawn Fraser banned from competitions for many years?
   a. She stole a flag from the Emperor's Palace at the Tokyo Olympics.
   b. She tested positive for drugs.
   c. She was a 'man' participating as a woman.

2. What is a leveret?
   a. A machine to lift heavy weight
   b. The young of a hare
   c. A remote control

3. Euphemistically, what is a 'marble orchard'?
   a. A shop which sells coloured playing marbles
   b. A graveyard, because of the marble tombstones
   c. A toilet decorated with glazed tiles

4. In India, if the Green Revolution referred to grains, and the White Revolution to milk, what did the Blue Revolution refer to?
   a. Tourism
   b. Production of fish
   c. Production of Indigo

5. What was the Bombay Pentangular?
   a. The five-storied Kapoor home
   b. A pre-Independence cricket tournament
   c. The five top film studios before Independence

CONFIDENCE ROUND

1. What do the number of dots on all six faces of a dice add up to?
2. Which religious place is famous for its Assi and Rewan Ghats: Sarnath or Varanasi?
3. In which country was Florence Nightingale born?
4. What is a four-letter word for a killer whale?
5. What is the STD code for New Delhi?
6. Which comet is named after a contemporary of Sir Isaac Newton?
7. Against which team did Steve Waugh make his Test debut: England or India?
8. When Jacob and Wilhelm first published them, they

were called *Children's and Household Tales*. How are these stories better known today?

9. Who was the leading lady in M.F. Hussain's *Meenaxi: A Tale of Three Cities*?

10. The sound of an elephant can be associated with which musical instrument?

WHAT'S THE WORD

Set 1

1. The characters Gru and Dr Nefario appear in which animated film series?

2. The FIFA Congress in Barcelona in 1929 assigned which country as the first host country of the FIFA World Cup: Bolivia or Uruguay?

3. Which variety of kebab was apparently invented by a highly skilled chef for a toothless Nawab of Lucknow: Shami kebab or Galouti kebab?

4. Where do the Wallace's flying frogs live almost exclusively: trees or oceans?

5. The name of which continent starts with the fifth letter of the alphabet?

6. In Indian railways, what does the letter 'R' in 'RAC' stand for?

7. What is the word?

Set 2

1. What does 'D' in the title 'D. Litt' stand for: doctor or director?

2. Which of these has a milk base: yoghurt or shikanji?

3. Hoshangabad and Jabalpur are situated on the banks

of which river?

4. The name of which animal is a Spanish word meaning 'little armored one'?
5. In the human body, striated, cardiac and smooth are all types of_____
6. Which epic by Homer deals with the wanderings of Odysseus after the fall of Troy?
7. What is the word?

Set 3

1. Which of these comes before the official name of Australia: Commonwealth or Republic?
2. Which of these cities is in Rajasthan: Udaipur or Ooty?
3. What lens would your grandfather use to correct his short sightedness: concave or convex?
4. Which niece of Rishi Kapoor made her debut opposite Abhishek Bachchan: Kareena Kapoor or Karishma Kapoor?
5. Which small word describes 'a pole with a blade used for rowing or steering a boat'?
6. Which is a citrus fruit: orange or banana?
7. What is the word?

Set 4

1. Ricky Ponting's nickname is Punter: agree or disagree?
2. Normally, in a pack of fifty-two playing cards, how many kings would you find?
3. What are Old Glory and Jolly Roger names of: flags or birds?

4. Quito is the capital of which country?
5. What is a rag doll made of?
6. What is an abnormally rabid heart rate called: tachycardia or thoracotomy?
7. What is the word?

Set 5

1. Which word describes 'a member of a sports team in their first full season': rookie or cookie?
2. Asmara is the capital of which country: Eritrea or Libya?
3. Which is the Maori word for 'peaks on the back': tarantula or tuatara?
4. Who look the same: fraternal twins or identical twins?
5. Which word derived from the Latin word for 'new' describes 'a star showing a sudden large increase of brightness'?
6. In many countries, what is the first day of the fourth month of the Gregorian calendar called?
7. What is the word?

MATHS AND IQ

1. Simplify this: The day before day after the day after the day before yesterday.
2. Fill in the blanks with either addition, subtraction, multiplication or division to figure out the correct answer. Go sequentially from left to right without following BODMAS.

6		9		7		95	=	10

3. Does the last statement follow the first two?

    a.   Marion is an Italian.
    b.   Marion sings beautifully.
    c.   All Italians sing beautifully.
4. Mr and Mrs Smith had seven sons. Each had a sister. How many people were there in the Smith family?
5. Fill in the blanks with either addition, subtraction, multiplication or division to figure out the correct answer. Go sequentially from left to right without following BODMAS.

50		15		5		1	=	12

VOCABULARY

1. Rearrange the letters of the word 'THROW' to get a word meaning value.
2. Rearrange the letters of the word 'ALSO' to find an Asian country.
3. Rearrange the letters of the word 'NEST' to get a kind of gun.
4. Read the word 'DESSERTS' (as in puddings) backwards, what word do you get?
5. Read the word 'YAM' backwards to get the name of a month.

SPEED

1. If tea is made from leaves, what is coffee made from?
2. What is the study of flags called?
3. Wales is a part of United Kingdom: serious or joking?
4. How many years are there in three decades?
5. In the acronym ESP, what does 'E' stand for?

6. Who created Sherlock Holmes: P.D. James or Arthur Conan Doyle?
7. The mridangam is a wind, percussion or stringed instrument?
8. What does 'merci' mean when translated from French to English?
9. How many seconds are there in a day?
10. Who was evil: Dr Jekyll or Mr Hyde?

ANSWERS

TAKE YOUR PICK
1. None
2. Chandragupta II
3. Dhanwantari
4. Computer. It is a small ball that is set in a holder, and can be rotated by hand to move a cursor on a computer screen.
5. Manhattan Island
6. Coriander
7. Uganda
8. West Bengal
9. Atlas
10. *Awara*

WHAT'S THE QUESTION

1. How would you express the number 1090 in Roman numerals?
2. Who was Babur?
3. What is the term used to describe the process of caring for and beautifying the feet?
4. Who was Dushala?
5. Who were Quasimodo's three gargoyle friends in the Walt Disney film *The Hunchback of Notre Dame*?
6. What is the *Mona Lisa*?
7. Name the most northerly pass that connects Pakistan and Afghanistan.

8. Who was the first US astronaut to orbit the Earth?
9. Who was Jawaharlal Nehru?
10. What is the medical term for baldness?

MIXED BAG

1. Balabhadr (Balarama, Baladeva)
2. China
3. Rajiv Gandhi
4. Scamper
5. Mumbai
6. Kiwi
7. Alexander Dityatin
8. The carved heads of former US presidents George Washington, Thomas Jefferson, Abraham Lincoln and Theodore Roosevelt at Mount Rushmore
9. M.S. Subbulakshmi
10. *Pather Panchali*

SPOT THE ANSWER

1. She stole a flag from the Emperor's palace at the Tokyo Olympics
2. The young of a hare
3. A graveyard, because of the marble tombstones
4. Production of fish
5. A pre-Independence cricket tournament

CONFIDENCE ROUND
1. Twenty-one
2. Varanasi

3. Italy
4. Orca
5. 011
6. Haley's Comet, after Edmund Haley
7. India
8. Grimms' Fairy Tales
9. Tabu
10. The trumpet

WHAT'S THE WORD

Set 1

1. *Despicable Me*
2. Uruguay
3. Shami kebab
4. Trees
5. Europe
6. Reservation
7. DUSTER

Set 2

1. Doctor
2. Yoghurt
3. Narmada
4. Armadillo
5. Muscles
6. *Odyssey*
7. DYNAMO

Set 3

1. Commonwealth

2. Udaipur
3. Concave
4. Kareena Kapoor
5. Oar
6. Orange
7. CUCKOO

Set 4

1. Agree
2. Four
3. Flags
4. Ecuador
5. Cloth
6. Tachycardia
7. AFFECT

Set 5

1. Rookie
2. Eritrea
3. Tuatara
4. Identical twins
5. Nova
6. April Fools' Day
7. RETINA

MATHS AND IQ

1. Yesterday
2. | 6 | Plus | 9 | Multiply | 7 | Minus | 95 | = | 10 |
3. No
4. Ten (Each brother had the same sister.)

5.

| 50 | Plus | 15 | Divided | 5 | Minus | 1 | = | 12 |

VOCABULARY

1. WORTH
2. LAOS
3. STEN
4. STRESSED
5. MAY

SPEED

1. Beans
2. Vexillology
3. Serious
4. Thirty
5. Extra (Extra Sensory Perception)
6. Arthur Conan Doyle
7. Percussion
8. Thank you
9. 86400
10. Mr Hyde

SET 7

TAKE YOUR PICK

1. Which is the only giant planet whose equator is nearly at right angles to its orbit?
   a. Mars
   b. Jupiter
   c. Uranus

2. The archeological remains of which institution is found in the vicinity of a village called 'Bara Gaon' in the eastern part of India?
   a. Nalanda University
   b. Taxila University
   c. Ujjain Sun Temple

3. In the Mahabharata, which grandson of Pandu died in warfare when he was trapped in a 'Chakravyuha'?
   a. Abhimanyu
   b. Prativindhya
   c. Yaudheya

4. In Buddhism, what among these does the 'swastika' signify?
   a. Buddha's feet or footprints
   b. Teachings of Buddha
   c. Signature of Buddha

5. Which style of cooking shares its name with the second largest province of China?
   a. Hunan
   b. Szechwan
   c. Shandong

6. Sri Jayawardenepura Kotte is the legislative and judicial capital of which country?
   a. Maldives
   b. Sri Lanka
   c. Seychelles

7. Shakti Sthal is the samadhi of which prime minister of India?
   a. Jawaharlal Nehru
   b. Charan Singh
   c. Indira Gandhi

8. 'Yakshagana' is a traditional theatre form of which Indian state?
   a. Maharashtra
   b. Andhra Pradesh
   c. Karnataka

9. Which famous author's original name was Charles Lutwidge Dodgson?
   a   Enid Blyton
   b. Lewis Carroll
   c. Charles Dickens

10. In which film has Michelle McNally's story been

memorably told?
a. *Black*
b. *Family*
c. *Hum Tum*

WHAT'S THE QUESTION

1. Isthmus
2. Ornithology
3. Moat
4. Château
5. In India, it is popularly known as imli.
6. Tinker Bell's friend who never grew up
7. Gossima and then ping-pong
8. A comic-strip character whose car is registered with the number 313.
9. Louis and Auguste Lumière
10. The Potala Palace is the winter residence of this religious leader.

MIXED BAG

1. The capital of which Indian state is named after Ananthan, the cosmic serpent with a thousand heads?
2. Which famous dancer founded Kalakshetra at Adyar in Chennai?
3. Work out the four-letter name of this animal. The first two letters make a verb. The first three an Indian state. The last three a cereal plant and the last two a preposition.
4. Which famous monument is the tomb of Muhammad

Adil Shah?

5. Who was the commander of the Pandava forces during the battle of Kurukshetra?

6. In 1865, the first edition of which book by an English mathematician was withdrawn because of bad printing?

7. Spiridon Louis won the marathon gold in the first modern Olympics at Athens in 1896. Which country did he represent?

8. The name of which country was coined by Choudhry Rahmat Ali and is said to be an acronym formed from Punjab, Afghania, Kashmir, Sind and Baluchistan?

9. I played a blind school principal in the 1980 film *Sparsh* and a professor in the 1993 film *Sir*. Who am I?

10. Which cuisine, introduced during the reign of Nawab Asaf-ud-Daulah, literally means 'choking off the steam'?

SPOT THE ANSWER

1. Arabica and Robusta are two main varieties of what?
   a. Horse
   b. Coffee
   c. Biryani

2. What became an Olympic event in 1912 at the Stockholm Games?
   a. Women's Swimming
   b. Canoe sprinting
   c. Basketball

3. What is fly ash?
   a. Mosquitoes killed by repellents
   b. Aishwarya Rai's private helicopter
   c. Small dark flecks produced by the burning of powdered coal or other materials

4. Who founded the 'Heal the World Foundation', for the safety, health and development of children?
   a. Hillary Clinton
   b. Laloo Prasad Yadav
   c. Michael Jackson

5. Which famous Indian's ashes were lying in the main branch of the State Bank of India in Cuttack since 1950?
   a. Dr S. Radhakrishnan
   b. K.L. Saigal
   c. Mahatma Gandhi

CONFIDENCE ROUND

1. Which of these is a steamed dumpling filled with meat or vegetables: momo or pasta?
2. In India, which is the highest peacetime gallantry award: Param Vir Chakra or Ashok Chakra?
3. Normally, what happens to its temperature when an animal goes into hibernation?
4. Who was a Pakistani fast bowler: Danish Kaneria or Mohammad Sami?
5. Are horses herbivorous or carnivorous?
6. The famous Gahirmatha beach in Odisha is located

on which Indian coast: east or west?

7. Which Paul wrote the bestselling book *The Population Bomb*: Ehrlich or Wood?
8. What kind of tube sticks out from the front of a kettle: snout, spout or tout?
9. Encephalitis is a disease that affects the brain. Which part of your body is affected when you have hepatitis?
10. Who is an expert at conducting an orchestra: Zakir Hussain or Zubin Mehta?

WHAT'S THE WORD

Set 1

1. Florence Nightingale was born in Florence: agree or disagree?
2. The name of which animal comes from the Hindi words for 'blue' and 'cow'?
3. Which is the largest city in Australia?
4. Who wrote the famous poem *Daffodils*?
5. Which part of the human body has photoreceptors?
6. Which Indian president was the president of the Indian National Congress in 1934, 1939 and 1947?
7. What is the word?

Set 2

1. The Cardamom Hills are a part of the Western Ghats: agree or disagree?
2. In Hindi, which spice is known as *saunf*: fennel or fenugreek?
3. On which day do tableau presentations normally take place in front of VIPs in New Delhi: Republic Day or

Independence Day?

4. Fe is the symbol of which chemical element?
5. In navigation or surveying, which is the primary device to find a direction on Earth?
6. Which eleven-letter word starting with 'A' is a magician's favourite word?
7. What is the word?

Set 3

1. In India, what did the Blue Mutiny refer to: indigo or rice?
2. Ne is the chemical symbol of which element?
3. All planets in the solar system are named after gods of Greek mythology: serious or joking?
4. Where is the archaeological site Sarnath located: Madhya Pradesh or Uttar Pradesh?
5. Which train first ran between Delhi and Howrah in 1969: Duronto or Rajdhani?
6. Which worm is also called angleworm?
7. What is the word?

Set 4

1. Spaniels are so called because they apparently originated in Spain: serious or joking?
2. In the abbreviation www, what does the third 'w' stand for: wide or web?
3. Which Southeast Asian country was formerly known as Dutch East Indies?
4. Which spice is the dried, cleaned and polished rhizome of *Curcuma longa*: tamarind or turmeric?
5. Which famous leader was Rajmohan Gandhi's

maternal grandfather?

6. The Greek word for sun, *helios*, was used in naming which element?
7. What is the word?

Set 5

1. As a prefix, 'sub' means under or over?
2. Which blood cells carry oxygen to body tissues: red blood cells or white blood cells?
3. Which continent has both the highest and the lowest points on the surface of the Earth?
4. Who became the president of South Africa in 1994?
5. In mythology, Shakuni was Duryodhana's uncle or grandfather?
6. What word connects the following clues: dwarfs, wonders and continents?
7. What is the word?

MATHS AND IQ

1. How much mud is there in a hole 1 foot by 2.5 feet by 3.75 feet?
2. Gloria has twelve right-hand gloves and fifteen left-hand gloves in a drawer. How many gloves should she take out to be sure of taking out at least one of each hand?
3. Fill in the blanks with either addition, subtraction, multiplication or division to figure out the correct answer. Go sequentially from left to right without following BODMAS.

5		2		50		4	=	15

4. Find the next number in the sequence: 8, 15, 29, 57, _____

5. Fill in the blanks with either addition, subtraction, multiplication or division to figure out the correct answer. Go sequentially from left to right without following BODMAS.

45		5		10		13	=	6

VOCABULARY

1. Rearrange the letters of the word 'POST' to put an end to motion.
2. Rearrange the letters of the word 'CARPEL' to get a word for goods wrapped up in a package.
3. Rearrange the letters of the word 'DUST' to find a place where horses are bred.
4. Read the word 'STRAW' backwards to get a hard, rough growth on the surface of the skin.
5. Read the word 'EMIT' backwards to get a unit of measurement.

SPEED

1. In *The Thousand and One Nights*, who recounts his adventures on seven voyages: Sindbad or Aladdin?
2. Which country is referred to as Druk-Yul meaning 'Land of the Thunder Dragon' in their local language?
3. Is the scapula above or below the femur?
4. How long will it take a car to travel 150 km at an

average speed of 30 kmph?

5. Who was the captain of the 1983 team which won the Cricket World Cup for India?

6. How many legs does a camera tripod have?

7. Bats hang upside down when asleep: serious or joking?

8. How many metres make a kilometre: 100 or 1,000?

9. Which brothers achieved the first powered, sustained, and controlled airplane flight?

10. In Indian history, who was the famous wife of Raja Gangadhar Rao?

ANSWERS

TAKE YOUR PICK

1. Uranus
2. Nalanda University
3. Abhimanyu
4. Buddha's feet or footprints
5. Szechwan
6. Sri Lanka
7. Indira Gandhi
8. Karnataka
9. Lewis Carroll
10. *Black*

WHAT'S THE QUESTION

1. What do you call a narrow strip of land with sea on either side, joining two larger masses of land?
2. What do you call the scientific study of birds?
3. What do you call a trench filled with water that surrounds a castle?
4. What is a large French country house or castle called?
5. What is the Indian (Hindi) name for tamarind?
6. Who is Peter Pan?
7. What was the original name of table tennis?
8. Who is Donald Duck?
9. Who were the creators of the first motion picture?

10. Who is Dalai Lama?

MIXED BAG

1. Kerala
2. Rukmini Devi Arundale
3. Goat
4. Gol Gumbaz
5. Dhrishtadyumna. He was Draupadi's brother.
6. *Alice's Adventures in Wonderland*
7. Greece
8. Pakistan
9. Naseeruddin Shah
10. Dum pukht

SPOT THE ANSWER

1. Coffee
2. Women's Swimming
3. Small dark flecks produced by the burning of powdered coal or other materials
4. Michael Jackson
5. Mahatma Gandhi. They were finally immersed in the holy Sangam in Allahabad.

CONFIDENCE ROUND

1. Momo
2. Ashok Chakra
3. It decreases
4. Mohammad Sami

5. Herbivorous
6. East
7. Ehrlich
8. Spout
9. The liver
10. Zubin Mehta

WHAT'S THE WORD

Set 1

1. Agree
2. Nilgai
3. Sydney
4. William Wordsworth
5. Eyes
6. Rajendra Prasad
7. ANSWER

Set 2

1. Agree
2. Fennel
3. Republic Day
4. Iron
5. Compass
6. Abracadabra
7. AFRICA

Set 3

1. Indigo
2. Neon
3. Joking

4. Uttar Pradesh
5. Rajdhani Express
6. Earthworm
7. INJURE

Set 4

1. Serious
2. Web
3. Indonesia
4. Turmeric
5. C. Rajagopalachari
6. Helium
7. SWITCH

Set 5

1. Under
2. Red blood cells
3. Asia
4. Nelson Mandela
5. Uncle
6. Seven
7. URANUS

MATHS AND IQ

1. There is no mud in a hole.
2. Sixteen
3.

5	Multiply	2	Plus	50	Divide	4	=	15

4. 99 (Beginning with 7, even multiples of 7 are added to the previous number to get the next number.)

5.

| 45 | Divide | 5 | Plus | 10 | Minus | 13 | = | 6 |

VOCABULARY

1. STOP
2. PARCEL
3. STUD
4. WARTS
5. TIME

SPEED

1. Sindbad
2. Bhutan
3. Above
4. Five hours
5. Kapil Dev
6. Three
7. Serious
8. 1,000
9. The Wright brothers
10. Rani Lakshmibai/Rani of Jhansi

SET 8

TAKE YOUR PICK

1. Fill in the blank: the wheel and axle, the lever, the ramp, the screw and the pulley are all_____ machines.
   a. Simple
   b. Turbine
   c. Mechanical components

2. According to Hindu mythology, which snake killed Parikshit?
   a. Kaliya
   b. Takshak
   c. Ananta

3. In which city can you find the mausoleum of Arjumand Bano Begum?
   a. Delhi
   b. Agra
   c. Aurangabad

4. What is described in the Oxford English Dictionary as 'an Indian sweet made from a mixture of flour, sugar, and shortening, which is shaped into a ball'?
   a. Rasgulla
   b. Laddu
   c. Balushahi

5. The name of which city comes from two words meaning 'market for areca nut' in the local language?
   a. Guwahati
   b. Kohima
   c. Itanagar

6. In geometry, which figure gets its name from the Greek word for 'table'?
   a. Rhombus
   b. Square
   c. Trapezeum

7. Who wrote the science fiction classic *Rendezvous with Rama*?
   a. Arthur C. Clarke
   b. Ray Bradbury
   c. H.G. Wells

8. The life of which deity makes up the most common theme of Pahadi paintings?
   a. Buddha
   b. Narada
   c. Krishna

9. Who was the first woman to be appointed the governor of Uttar Pradesh?
   a. Sucheta Kripalani
   b. Sarojini Naidu
   c. Vijaya Lakshmi Pandit

10. 15 August 2005 marked the thirtieth anniversary of

which path-breaking film?

a. *Deewar*
b. *Mughal-e-Azam*
c. *Sholay*

WHAT'S THE QUESTION

1. This fictional character has been played by Sean Connery, David Niven, George Lazenby and Roger Moore on screen.
2. According to the Western zodiac, the name of this constellation means 'goat-horned' in Latin.
3. 'Mitrabhed' and 'Mitralabh' are two of the five chapters of this famous work by Vishnu Sharma.
4. 8,611 metres, making it the second highest mountain in the world.
5. This element was so named because Cyprus was the chief source.
6. Filigree
7. Mintonette
8. A naked winged boy with a bow and arrows
9. The Swedish Academy, The Norwegian Committee, The Royal Swedish Academy of Sciences and The Assembly at Karolinska Institutet
10. Gowalia Tank Maidan, Mumbai (now called August Kranti Maidan)

MIXED BAG

1. In 1590, the Portuguese first sighted the island of Taiwan. What did they name it?

2. For which famous monument is Ustad Isa credited?
3. Which is the only member of the cat family to live in groups called prides?
4. What is common to cheddar, mozzarella, edam and camembert?
5. The Rigveda Samhita is divided into ten books. What are the books called?
6. What is the main ingredient in a finger bowl?
7. In which capital city would you find the famous Temple of the Emerald Buddha?
8. In World War II, what was code-named 'Operation Barbarossa'?
9. We were born as Arthur Stanley Jefferson and Oliver Norvell Hardy. We are a famous comedy pair. How are we better known?
10. Who was the first woman to fly solo across the Atlantic Ocean?

SPOT THE ANSWER

1. The Incas had no form of writing, instead, they had relay runners conveying messages by carrying what they called 'quipus'. What were quipus?
   a. Double-sided mirrors
   b. Knotted designs of human hair
   c. Colour-coded arrangements of knotted threads

2. Which king called himself 'Devanampiya Piyadasi' or 'beloved of the gods and handsome in looks'?
   a. Ashoka
   b. Prithviraj Chauhan

   c.   Maharana Pratap

3. Of what are A4 and B5 sizes?
   a.   Diamond
   b.   CD-Roms
   c.   Paper

4. In 1804, the Cathedral of Notre Dame in Paris witnessed the crowning ceremony of...
   a.   Alexander the Great
   b.   Napoleon Bonaparte
   c.   Louis XVI

5. Why is House 54 on University Avenue, in Rangoon, a big tourist attraction?
   a.   It was the house where Aung San Suu Kyi was kept under house arrest
   b.   It is the site of the world's largest pagoda
   c.   Lord Mountbatten's grave is located there

CONFIDENCE ROUND

1. Marble cakes are actually made of marble: serious or joking?
2. Which Leo wrote the books *Anna Karenina* and *War and Peace*?
3. If the flamenco is a dance form, what is a flamingo?
4. In Hindu mythology, who was Pandu's wife: Kunti or Gandhari?
5. Which tiny particle has about the same mass as a proton: neutron or electron?

6. Which Indian state is bordered by Pakistan and the states of Rajasthan, Madhya Pradesh and Maharashtra?
7. Which actress made her debut in the film *Pardes*: Shilpa Shetty or Mahima Choudhary?
8. Are ants classified as social, anti-social or socialist insects?
9. The Vidarbha Cricket Association Stadium is located in which city in Maharashtra: Ahmedabad or Nagpur?
10. Which part of the word 'bifocals' means two?

WHAT'S THE WORD

Set 1

1. Which of these European nations is an island: Georgia or Malta?
2. Clementines, tangerines and cara caras are types of which fruit?
3. Which scientist is more famous for his works on gravity: Newton or Herschel?
4. Which director would you associate with the films *Hero No. 1* and *Coolie No. 1*: David Dhawan or Mahesh Bhatt?
5. Who is the author of the book *Wings of Fire*?
6. Which part of the egg is also called deutoplasm?
7. What is the word?

Set 2

1. Which grow faster: fingernails or toenails?
2. Which boy's name is spoken in radio communication to convey that the message has been understood:

Roger or Rover?

3. In which continent does the River Po flow: Africa or Europe?
4. Which chemical element was first identified as a unique element in 1751 by Baron Axel Fredrik Cronstedt: Nickel or Copper?
5. Which spice is called *elaichi* in Hindi: cardamom or mustard?
6. Which Mughal ruler was also called Nasir-al-Din Muhammad?
7. What is the word?

Set 3

1. In *Gulliver's Travels*, what was Gulliver's first name: Lemuel or Samuel?
2. Hyder Ali was Tipu Sultan's father: agree or disagree?
3. Which of these is a marsupial: wombat or armadillo?
4. In *Tintin* comics, who was the Abominable Snowman?
5. Which cricket stadium is named after Lord Auckland's sisters: Eden Gardens or Green Park?
6. In which state of india is the Hawa Mahal located?
7. What is the word?

Set 4

1. In which of these films have Hema Malini and Amitabh Bachchan appeared together: *Baghban* or *Kal Ho Naa Ho*?
2. The auditory ossicles are located in which organ of the human body?
3. Which commentator has not played Test cricket: Ravi Shastri or Harsha Bhogle?

4. Which state is larger in terms of area: Arunachal Pradesh or Manipur?
5. In Tibet, which breed of dog is called 'abso seng kye'?
6. How many angles does a pentagon have?
7. What is the word?

Set 5

1. Which fruit is commonly used as flavouring in golgappas: tamarind or mango?
2. Which Indian bowler made his Test debut in Australia: L. Balaji or Irfan Pathan?
3. What is the first name of the Indian painter M.F. Hussain: Mian or Maqbool?
4. The Ganges flows through Bihar or Tamil Nadu?
5. Which is the third planet from the sun and the fifth largest in our solar system?
6. Under Peter the Great, which country was proclaimed an empire in 1721: Italy or Russia?
7. What is the word?

MATHS AND IQ

1. Rearrange the letters and find the odd one: EMEPLT QUOMSE EHOSU HURHCC
2. Ravi's watch is ten minutes slow, though he thinks it is five minutes fast. Rohan's watch is five minutes fast though he thinks it is ten minutes slow. They both plan to catch a train at 4 p.m. Who gets their first: Ravi or Rohan?
3. Fill in the blanks with either addition, subtraction, multiplication or division to figure out the correct

answer. Go sequentially from left to right without following BODMAS.

| 13 | | 17 | | 28 | | 3 | = | 6 |

4. Assuming the truth of these sentences
   (a) Yellow dogs are live animals.
   (b) All live animals need food.
   Which of the following sentences is true?
   1) A dog is yellow because it needs food.
   2) All yellow dogs need food.
   3) Certain yellow dogs do not need food.
   4) Some yellow dogs are not live animals.
5. Fill in the blanks with either addition, subtraction, multiplication or division to figure out the correct answer. Go sequentially from left to right without following BODMAS.

| 3 | | 97 | | 10 | | 6 | = | 15 |

VOCABULARY

1. Rearrange the letters of the word 'GOAT' to get a Roman costume.
2. Rearrange the letters of the word 'CARE' to get a unit of land measurement.
3. Rearrange the letters of the word 'GAIN' to get a Hindu god.
4. Read the word 'FLOW' backwards to get an animal's name.
5. Read the word 'ABLE' backwards to get where Napoleon was exiled.

SPEED

1. Which actor was affectionately called 'Kaka': Rajesh Khanna or Shammi Kapoor?
2. Who was the 'chief' of the losing team at the Battle of Plassey?
3. It is called turmeric in English. What is it called in Hindi?
4. If you consume 0.264 gallons of milk, how many litres would you have consumed?
5. Which four-letter word represents the pointed top of a mountain?
6. Which teeth of yours sounds like a dog?
7. How many sides does a hexagon have?
8. Which country is the second largest producer of silk?
9. What is the state tree of Kerala?
10. Which satellite orbited the Earth first: Sputnik or Explorer I?

ANSWERS

TAKE YOUR PICK

1. Simple
2. Takshak
3. Agra
4. Laddu
5. Guwahati
6. Trapezeum
7. Arthur C. Clarke
8. Krishna
9. Sarojini Naidu
10. *Sholay*. It was released on 15 August 1975.

WHAT'S THE QUESTION

1. Who is James Bond?
2. What is Capricorn?
3. What is *Panchatantra*?
4. What is the height of the mountain K2 or Godwin Austen?
5. What is copper?
6. What term is used to describe the application of gold or silver on a surface in a fine pattern?
7. What was the original name of volleyball?
8. In Roman mythology, how is Cupid (the god of love) depicted?

9. Which organisations are responsible for awarding the Nobel Prizes every year?
10. Where did Gandhiji give his 'Quit India' call during the freedom movement?

MIXED BAG

1. Formosa
2. The Taj Mahal
3. Lion
4. All of these are varieties of cheese.
5. Mandalas
6. Water
7. Bangkok
8. The German attack on the (former) USSR in 1941
9. Laurel and Hardy
10. Amelia Earhart

SPOT THE ANSWER

1. Colour-coded arrangements of knotted threads. The colours of the cords, the way the cords are connected together, the relative placement of the cords, the spaces between the cords, the types of knots on the individual cords, and the relative placement of the knots are all part of theological-numerical recording.
2. Ashoka
3. Paper. In the ISO paper size system, all pages have a height-to-width ratio of the square root of two (1:1.4142).
4. Napoleon Bonaparte

5. It was the house where Aung San Suu Kyi was kept under house arrest. She won the Nobel Peace prize in 1991.

CONFIDENCE ROUND

1. Joking. It is a cake with a streaked or mottled appearance achieved by very lightly blending light and dark batter.
2. Leo Tolstoy
3. A bird
4. Kunti
5. Neutron
6. Gujarat
7. Mahima Choudhary
8. Social
9. Nagpur
10. Bi

WHAT'S THE WORD

Set 1

1. Malta
2. Orange
3. Newton
4. David Dhawan
5. A.P.J. Abdul Kalam
6. Yolk
7. MONDAY

Set 2

1. Fingernails
2. Roger
3. Europe
4. Nickel
5. Cardamom
6. Humayun
7. FRENCH

Set 3

1. Lemuel
2. Agree
3. Wombat
4. Yeti
5. Eden Gardens
6. Rajasthan
7. LAWYER

Set 4

1. *Baghban*
2. Ear
3. Harsha Bhogle
4. Arunachal Pradesh
5. Lhasa Apso
6. Five
7. BEHALF

Set 5

1. Tamarind
2. Irfan Pathan
3. Maqbool

4. Bihar
5. Earth
6. Russia
7. TIMBER

MATHS AND IQ

1. EHOSU (HOUSE). The others are public places of worship—TEMPLE, CHURCH, MOSQUE.
2. Rohan. He came earlier as his watch was fast.
3.

| 13 | Plus | 17 | Minus | 28 | Multiply | 3 | = | 6 |

4. All yellow dogs need food.
5.

| 3 | Plus | 97 | Minus | 10 | Divide | 6 | = | 15 |

VOCABULARY

1. TOGA
2. ACRE
3. AGNI
4. WOLF
5. ELBA

SPEED

1. Rajesh Khanna
2. Siraj-ud-daulah
3. *Haldi*
4. One litre
5. Peak
6. Canine
7. Six

8. India
9. Coconut palm
10. Sputnik

SET 9

TAKE YOUR PICK

1. Which fabric was introduced by Sir H.B. Lumsden and W. Hodson in 1848 for the uniforms of British colonial troops in India?
   a. Khaki
   b. Denim
   c. Corduroy

2. In Hindu mytholgy, who cursed Krishna that he would be killed by trickery?
   a. Kunti
   b. Gandhari
   c. Karna

3. M.K. Gandhi lived in a farm in South Africa named after a famous Russian novelist. Name the author.
   a. Leo Tolstoy
   b. Mark Twain
   c. Charles Dickens

4. Haflong is the only hill station of…
   a. Manipur
   b. Assam
   c. Meghalaya

5. Thomson seedless, bangalore blue, anab-e-shahi are the major varieties of which fruit in India?
   a. Grapes
   b. Oranges
   c. Litchis

6. In which book would you come across the floating island of Laputa and the land of the Houyhnhnms?
   a. *Robinson Crusoe*
   b. *Kidnapped*
   c. *Gulliver's Travels*

7. Which Indian dance form traces its traditions to the Mahari and the Gotipua traditions?
   a. Kathak
   b. Kathakali
   c. Odissi

8. Who among these advises the Government of India on legal matters?
   a. Attorney General
   b. Speaker of the Lok Sabha
   c. Governor of Reserve Bank of India

9. In 1976, in which catgeory did *Sholay* win its only Filmfare Award?
   a. Best Film
   b. Best Director
   c. Best Editing

10. Which are the only big cats to have a tuft or a bunch

of hair at the end of their tail?
   a. Lions
   b. Tigers
   c. Jaguars

WHAT'S THE QUESTION

1. It is the currency of UAE.
2. La Marseillaise
3. The Golden Hind
4. Merci beaucoup
5. This theory explains that the universe began with a big explosion.
6. Green Goblin
7. Creutzfeldt-Jakob disease
8. A book called *Our Films, Their Films*
9. A painting called *Guernica*
10. A ball that reaches the batsmen without bouncing

MIXED BAG

1. Which is the southernmost capital city in the world?
2. In the Ramayana, which rakshasa was known as Jaya and served as Vishnu's gatekeeper at Vaikuntha?
3. A tigon is an offspring of a tiger and a lioness. What do you call the offspring of a lion and a tigress?
4. In which novel does Jean Valjean steal a loaf of bread and is imprisoned?
5. Upon completion in 1931, it was called the All India War Memorial. How do we know it today?
6. In 1974, who became the first Indian woman singer to

receive the Ramon Magsaysay award?

7. What was Abraham Lincoln referring to when he said, 'If I ever get a chance to hit that thing, I'll hit it hard'?

8. Which planet was predicted by a Frenchman named Le Verrier and an Englishman named John Adams?

9. Which Hollywood 1956 classic has the line, 'So let it be written, so it shall be done'?

10. In Kerala, if you are eating karimeen, what would you be eating?

SPOT THE ANSWER

1. The Chinese expression Kung Hei Fat Choi, means...
   a. Have a prosperous and happy new year
   b. Good luck for the quiz
   c. Happy birthday

2. In whose honour was 29 August chosen as National Sports Day in India?
   a. Milkha Singh's birthday
   b. Dhyan Chand's birthday
   c. Sunil Gavaskar's birthday

3. Some cough mixtures have the word 'linctus' in them, what is the origin of the term?
   a. Contains lime
   b. To be licked
   c. Contains linoleum

4. What is common to owls, aardvark, kiwi and bats?
   a. They all sleep on their backs.

b. They generally hunt at night.

c. They were all used as Olympic mascots.

5. What would a Chinese individual do with a wok?
   a. Burst it (Chinese cracker)
   b. Eat it (Dumpling)
   c. Cook in it (Chinese cooking vessel)

CONFIDENCE ROUND

1. Which of these places did an American reach first: the moon or space?
2. How many faces does a cuboid have?
3. Which Indian poet is also known as Bharatendu?
4. Bronze is an alloy traditionally composed of copper and _____.
5. Cabbages are always green in colour: serious or joking?
6. Who is younger: Sourav Ganguly or Mohammad Kaif?
7. Which of these is a reptile: iguana or echidna?
8. Which mountain range is broadly divided into the Canadian, Northern, Middle and Southern?
9. What does the 'O' in OPEC stand for?
10. Where did Vasco da Gama establish the first Portuguese factory: Cochin or Visakhapatnam?

WHAT'S THE WORD

Set 1

1. Which flower has a trumpet-shaped centre: dahlia or daffodil?

2. Which team has won more hockey gold medals in the Olympics: India or Pakistan?
3. Which epic means the 'great epic of the Bharata dynasty' in Sanskrit: Ramayana or Mahabharata?
4. Which city shares its name with a Trojan prince: Rome or Paris?
5. Who among these is a fictional character in the novel *Treasure Island*: Long John Silver or Fagin?
6. Which name has been applied to Arctic people by Europeans: eskimo or yeti?
7. What's the word?

Set 2

1. What is a marmoset: monkey or parrot?
2. Sneezing is a reflex action of the human body: agree or disagree?
3. Which actress made a guest appearance in *Kal Ho Naa Ho*: Rani Mukherjee or Madhuri Dixit?
4. Majuli, one of the largest riverine islands in the world, is on which river?
5. In Hindu mythology, who was Sumitra's son: Lakshmana or Bharata?
6. Which landmark is in Paris: Eiffel Tower or Colosseum?
7. What is the word?

Set 3

1. Which country is landlocked: Mali or South Africa?
2. Adam Gilchrist has captained Australia in Test cricket: agree or disagree?
3. Which is a form of dance: Tango or Tutu?

4. The health benefits and distinctive yellow colour of which spice come principally from a substance called curcumin?
5. Harpy, golden, bald and sea are different species of which bird?
6. Which four-letter name would you place before Pratap and after Jaspal?
7. What is the word?

Set 4

1. Which mythological character's name means 'Rama with an axe': Parashurama or Balaram?
2. Which continent has been called 'the Oldest Continent,' 'the Last of Lands,' and 'the Last Frontier'?
3. Who is the director of *Munnabhai MBBS*: Vidhu Vinod Chopra or Rajkumar Hirani?
4. Which of these animals can be found only on the island of Madagascar: aye-aye or aardvark?
5. Who is the spiritual head of the Tibetan Buddhists?
6. If you were facing north, which direction would your right hand point towards?
7. What is the word?

Set 5

1. Which moon would you find in the flag of Pakistan: crescent moon or full moon?
2. Which brother of Kishore Kumar worked as a lab assistant in Bombay Talkies?
3. In Maharashtra, which town is the site of Pandu and Chamar cave temples: Nasik or Ajanta?
4. Sirius, the brightest star in the night sky, is also called

the Cat Star or Dog Star?

5. Give me a six-letter word for a traditional story popularly regarded as historical but not authenticated.

6. Till 1990, Germany was divided into West Germany and which other part?

7. What is the word?

MATHS AND IQ

1. Why should a detective disbelieve this story? The spy entered the room, switched on the light, took a book from the shelf, and placed the secret note between pages 19 and 20.

2. Would it be cheaper to take one friend to the movies twice, or two friends at the same time?

3. Fill in the blanks with either addition, subtraction, multiplication or division to figure out the correct answer. Go sequentially from left to right without following BODMAS.

8		8		26		15	=	6

4. Which number comes next in the series: 3, 8, 15, 24, 35,_____?

5. Fill in the blanks with either addition, subtraction, multiplication or division to figure out the correct answer. Go sequentially from left to right without following BODMAS.

4		3		30		14	=	15

VOCABULARY

1. Rearrange the letters of the word 'FALSE' to find the name of some insects.
2. Rearrange the letters of the word 'SINK' to get a body organ.
3. Rearrange the letters of the word 'LAST' to find a compound of sodium.
4. Read the word 'SORE' to get the Greek god of love.
5. Read the word 'REPAID' backwards to get a baby's underpants.

SPEED

1. What fungus do bakers use?
2. Along the banks of which river is Agra located?
3. The word 'nasal' would describe which part of your body?
4. In cricket, how many runs are scored if a six is hit from a no ball?
5. Which of Batman's friends sound like a bird?
6. Besides Indira Gandhi, name another woman prime minister of India.
7. A stallion is a male horse: serious or joking?
8. Which is taller: the Qutb Minar or Charminar?
9. Who became the king of Kishkindha immediately after Bali's death?
10. Which key on a computer keyboard sounds like you have changed position?

ANSWERS

TAKE YOUR PICK

1. Khaki
2. Gandhari
3. Leo Tolstoy
4. Assam
5. Grapes
6. *Gulliver's Travels*
7. Odissi
8. Attorney General
9. Best Editing
10. Lions

WHAT'S THE QUESTION

1. What is dirham?
2. What is the French national anthem called?
3. In which ship did Francis Drake sail around the world?
4. What is the French equivalent of 'thank you very much'?
5. What is the Big Bang theory?
6. Name one of Spider-Man's enemies.
7. What is the human version of Mad Cow Disease called?
8. Name a famous book on films written by Satyajit Ray.

9. Name a famous painting by Pablo Picasso.
10. In cricket, what is full toss?

MIXED BAG

1. Wellington
2. Ravana
3. Liger
4. *Les Misérables*
5. India Gate
6. M.S. Subbulakshmi
7. Slavery
8. Neptune
9. *The Ten Commandments*
10. Fish

SPOT THE ANSWER

1. Have a prosperous and happy new year
2. Dhyan Chand's birthday. He was one of the greatest hockey players of all times.
3. To be licked. It is a Latin word.
4. They generally hunt at night.
5. Cook in it (Chinese cooking vessel)

CONFIDENCE ROUND

1. Moon
2. Six
3. Harishchandra
4. Tin

5. Joking
6. Mohammad Kaif
7. Iguana
8. Rockies
9. Organization
10. Cochin

WHAT'S THE WORD

Set 1

1. Daffodil
2. India
3. Mahabharata
4. Paris
5. Long John Silver
6. Eskimo
7. DIMPLE

Set 2

1. Monkey
2. Agree
3. Rani Mukherjee
4. Brahmaputra
5. Lakshmana
6. Eiffel Tower
7. MARBLE

Set 3

1. Mali
2. Agree
3. Tango

4. Turmeric
5. Eagle
6. Rana
7. MATTER

Set 4

1. Parashurama
2. Australia
3. Rajkumar Hirani
4. Aye-aye
5. Dalai Lama
6. East
7. PARADE

Set 5

1. Crescent moon
2. Ashok Kumar
3. Nasik
4. Dog Star
5. Legend
6. East Germany
7. CANDLE

MATHS AND IQ

1. In any book, pages 19 and 20 are two sides of the same page.
2. Two friends at the same time
3.

| 8 | Multiply | 8 | Plus | 26 | Divide | 15 | = | 6 |

4. 48 (Odd numbers from 5 onwards are added to get the next number.)

5. | 4 | Plus | 3 | Multiply | 30 | Divide | 14 | = | 15 |

VOCABULARY

1. FLEAS
2. SKIN
3. SALT
4. EROS
5. DIAPER

SPEED

1. Yeast
2. Yamuna
3. The nose
4. Seven
5. Robin
6. There are none.
7. Serious
8. The Qutb Minar
9. Sugriva
10. Shift

SET 10

TAKE YOUR PICK

1. In the hermitage of which sage was Shakuntala brought up?
   a. Kanva
   b. Agastya
   c. Dronacharya

2. According to Thomas Alva Edison, what was 1 per cent inspiration and 99 per cent perspiration?
   a. Genius
   b. Happiness
   c. His phonograph

3. Which leader did Mahatma Gandhi call the 'Prince among Patriots'?
   a. Netaji Subhas Chandra Bose
   b. Jawaharlal Nehru
   c. Vallabhbhai Patel

4. If you were a cartographer, what would you be studying?
   a. Maps
   b. Coins
   c. Postcards

5. Which nut is attached to a yellow or red pear-shaped false fruit?
   a. Almond
   b. Cashew nut
   c. Walnut

6. Which country's population consists mostly of Flemings and Walloons?
   a. Denmark
   b. Belgium
   c. Paraguay

7. In literature, which author used the pseudonym Isaac Bickerstaff?
   a. Mark Twain
   b. Jonathan Swift
   c. Roald Dahl

8. With which dance form would you associate the famous dancers Rukmini Devi Arundale and Yamini Krishnamurthy?
   a. Kathak
   b. Manipuri
   c. Bharatnatyam

9. Who appoints the Attorney General of India?
   a. The president
   b. The prime minister
   c. The chief justice of the Supreme Court

10. In 2008, who became the first Indian actor to receive the prestigious Malaysian title, 'Datuk'?

a. Aamir Khan
b. Ajay Devgn
c. Shah Rukh Khan

WHAT'S THE QUESTION

1. *With Malice towards One and All*
2. This Indian freedom fighter transformed Ganesha Chaturthi into a public event in Maharashtra.
3. Haradanahalli
4. Albert Mission School, Vinayak Mudali Street and Lawley Extension
5. The All England Lawn Tennis and Croquet Club
6. He played the role of Dennis the Menace in the 1993 film of the same name.
7. He created raga Priyadarshini in Indira Gandhi's honour.
8. Barchans
9. Chingachgook and his son Uncas
10. Epsilon, Theta, Iota, Sigma and Pi

MIXED BAG

1. Which social networking site was acquired by Facebook when it had just thirteen employees?
2. K2 or Godwin Austen is the world's second highest peak. To which range of mountains does it belong?
3. The Indian name of this snake is ajgar. What is its English name?
4. In 1985, who became the first unseeded player to win the Wimbledon Men's Singles tournament?

5. Which two words are inscribed below the abacus on the Emblem of India?

6. Name the German businessman who saved more than 1,000 Jews from Nazi camps and has been immortalized in an award-winning film?

7. Liquefied Petroleum Gas (LPG) is chemically odourless. Yet whenever this cooking gas leaks, we can smell it. Why?

8. Which infamous prison would you associate with 14 July 1789?

9. What is common to the following: banganapalli, safeda, langra, chausa and malda?

10. Fill in the missing word in these lines from a poem by Nissim Ezekiel: 'Thank God the _____ picked on me/ And spared my children.'

SPOT THE ANSWER

1. How did Ranjit Singh lose one of his eyes?
   a. Injury while playing polo
   b. Born with one eye
   c. Due to smallpox

2. Prince Philip is the president emeritus of which of these organisations?
   a. World Wildlife Fund
   b. World Wrestling Federation
   c. World Whale Foundation

3. Which collection of stories is also called *Alf laylah wa laylah*?

    a. *Arabian Nights*
    b. *Jataka Tales*
    c. *Panchatantra*

4. Who was the king of Japan during World War II?
    a. Ajinomoto
    b. Hirohito
    c. Akihito

5. The dog that would eventually evolve into Mickey Mouse's dog Pluto made his debut in The Chain Gang as a...
    a. Dachshund
    b. Mixed breed
    c. Bloodhound

CONFIDENCE ROUND

1. What would ache if you had a migraine?
2. What is pressed while changing gears: clutch or brake?
3. Abhimanyu was the son of Subhadra and which Pandava?
4. Blue, Green and Congo are different species of which bird: peacock or parrot?
5. Which of these rivers flows into the Bay of Bengal: Narmada or Godavari?
6. In Rudyard Kipling's *The Jungle Book*, what kind of a creature was Baloo?
7. With which letter do the names of most films directed by Rakesh Roshan start: 'K' or 'R'?
8. The official residence of the prime minister of India is

in New Delhi or Mumbai?

9. The name of which Olympic sport comes from a Latin word meaning 'belonging to a horseman'?

10. Which of these is chiefly used to make platinum alloys: iridium or radium?

WHAT'S THE WORD

Set 1

1. Gases that heat up the atmosphere by trapping sunlight are called greenhouse gases or redhouse gases?

2. Which dance form originated in eastern India: Odissi or Kathak?

3. In Scotland, what kind of a water body is a 'loch': sea or lake?

4. What was the name of a system of ethics founded by Akbar: *Din-i-Ilahi* or *Baburnama*?

5. Which actress is the sister of Ahana and the step sister of actor Bobby Deol?

6. Auckland is the largest urban area of which island nation?

7. What is the word?

Set 2

1. Raja Ravi Varma was a famous actor or painter?

2. Another term used for a lift is an escalator or an elevator?

3. Which of these is an Indian sweetmeat: rasmalai or rasam?

4. If P stands for Postal and N stands for Number, what

does 'I' in PIN stand for: India or Index?

5. Which famous leader was born in Cuttack on 23 January 1897?
6. In which north Indian state would you be if you were sightseeing in Dalhousie?
7. What's the word?

Set 3

1. Who was the successor to Chandragupta I, the ruler of the Gupta empire?
2. Which state capital comes administratively under Papum Pare district: Itanagar or Kohima?
3. Rajapuri, langra and dussehri are some of the varieties of which fruit?
4. Till date, which country has won the ICC Cricket World Cup only once: West Indies or Pakistan?
5. Hindu mythology portrays goddess Saraswati as being seated on which flower?
6. The name of which currency was chosen by the European Council meeting in Madrid in 1995?
7. What is the word?

Set 4

1. The sun is a star or a planet?
2. Which snake kills its victims using venom: cobra or python?
3. Sourav Ganguly is a left-handed or a right-handed bowler?
4. Amitabh Bachchan made his debut as an actor in *Saat Hindustani*: agree or disagree?
5. The name of which fruit comes from the Greek word

for 'large melon'?

6. Which eleven-letter word ending in 'ware' describes pots and dishes made of baked clay?

7. What is the word?

Set 5

1. Name Ralf Schumacher's brother who also competed in the same sport.

2. No two giraffes have the same pattern of spots: agree or disagree?

3. In the Ramayana, who was Kusha's mother?

4. Which of its world heritage sites does India share with Bangladesh: Sunderbans or Kaziranga National Park?

5. Who is the famous paternal grandmother of Rahul Gandhi?

6. F is the symbol of which chemical element?

7. What is the word?

MATHS AND IQ

1. A test has twenty questions. If Peter gets 80 per cent correct, how many did he miss?

2. Fill in the blanks with either addition, subtraction, multiplication or division to figure out the correct answer. Go sequentially from left to right without following BODMAS.

21		7		10		2	=	11

3. A zoo had 44 female and 36 male zebras. Which is the correct ratio of females to males?

4. Which number comes next in the series: 1, 1, 2, 3, 4, 9, 8, _____

5. Fill in the blanks with either addition, subtraction, multiplication or division to figure out the correct answer. Go sequentially from left to right without following BODMAS.

84		47		2		3	=	13

VOCABULARY

1. Rearrange the letters of the word 'TASTE' to find what Uttarakhand is.
2. Rearrange the letters of the word 'MARY' to find one of the wings of the armed forces.
3. Rearrange the letters of the word 'WENT' to find the name of an amphibian.
4. Read the word 'FLOG' backwards to get the name of a game.
5. Read the word 'MADE' backwards to get a town in Holland or hard cheese.

SPEED

1. What is the study or collection of coins, paper currency and medals called?
2. Who was the first American to go to space: Neil Armstrong or Alan Shepard?
3. On which part of your body might you wear pumps?
4. Who was president of the US immediately before Bill Clinton?
5. Workers are the only bees that most people ever see: serious or joking?
6. Which country hosted the 2000 Olympic Games?

7. How many sides does a heptagon have?
8. Which geometric instrument is used to draw arcs and circles?
9. The Hawaii Islands are a part of which country?
10. In *Raja Hindustani*, who played the role of the Aarti Sehgal?

ANSWERS

TAKE YOUR PICK

1. Kanva
2. Genius
3. Netaji Subhas Chandra Bose
4. Maps
5. Cashew nut
6. Belgium
7. Jonathan Swift
8. Bharatnatyam
9. The president
10. Shah Rukh Khan

WHAT'S THE QUESTION

1. What was the name of the popular column written by Khushwant Singh?
2. Who was Lokmanya Tilak?
3. What is the first name of Prime Minister Deve Gowda?
4. Name some famous landmarks in Malgudi, the fictional town created by R.K. Narayan.
5. What is the full name of the club that owns and governs the Wimbledon tennis tournament?
6. Who is Mason Gamble?
7. Who is Amjad Ali Khan?
8. What is a crescent-shaped sand dune called?

9. In the book of the same name, who were the last of the Mohicans?
10. Name some of the letters of the Greek alphabet.

MIXED BAG

1. Instagram
2. Karakoram
3. Python
4. Boris Becker
5. *Satyameva Jayate*
6. Oskar Schindler
7. The smell is deliberately added so that people can detect leaks.
8. Bastille
9. All of them are varieties of mangoes.
10. Scorpion

SPOT THE ANSWER

1. Due to smallpox
2. World Wildlife Fund
3. *Arabian Nights*
4. Hirohito
5. Bloodhound

CONFIDENCE ROUND

1. Your head
2. Clutch
3. Arjuna

4. Peacock
5. Godavari
6. Black bear
7. 'K'
8. New Delhi
9. Equestrian
10. Iridium

WHAT'S THE WORD

Set 1

1. Greenhouse gases
2. Odissi
3. Lake
4. *Din-i-Ilahi*
5. Esha Deol
6. New Zealand
7. GOLDEN

Set 2

1. Painter
2. Elevator
3. Rasmalai
4. Index
5. Subhas Chandra Bose
6. Himachal Pradesh
7. PERISH

Set 3

1. Samudragupta
2. Itanagar

3. Mango
4. Pakistan
5. Lotus
6. Euro
7. SIMPLE

Set 4

1. Star
2. Cobra
3. Right-handed
4. Agree
5. Pumpkin
6. Earthenware
7. SCRAPE

Set 5

1. Michael Schumacher
2. Agree
3. Sita
4. Sunderbans
5. Indira Gandhi
6. Fluorine
7. MASSIF

MATHS AND IQ

1. Four
2.

21	Divide	7	Plus	10	Minus	2	=	11

3. 11:9
4. 27 (Two consecutive series are present. In the first series, each number is multiplied by 2 and in the

second, by 3.)

5. | 84 | Minus | 47 | Plus | 2 | Divide | 3 | = | 13 |

VOCABULARY

1. STATE
2. ARMY
3. NEWT
4. GOLF
5. EDAM

SPEED

1. Numismatics
2. Alan Shepard
3. Feet. It is a type of shoe.
4. George H.W. Bush
5. Serious
6. Australia
7. Seven
8. Compass
9. The US
10. Karishma Kapoor

SET 11

TAKE YOUR PICK

1. In the Mahabharata, who was Nakula's mother?
   a. Kunti
   b. Madri
   c. Gandhari

2. Which element's chemical symbol Au derives from the Latin *aurum*, for Aurora the goddess of dawn?
   a. Silver
   b. Gold
   c. Platinum

3. For which monument were 20,000 workmen accommodated in a small town named Mumtazabad in the 1630s?
   a. Red Fort
   b. Taj Mahal
   c. Agra Fort

4. In 1917, 1944 and 1963, which organization had the unique distinction of being awarded the Nobel Peace Prize?
   a. Grameen Bank
   b. United Nations Children's Fund (UNICEF)
   c. The International Committee of the Red Cross

5. Akoori is a traditional dish of which community?
   a. Buddhists
   b. Parsis
   c. Jains

6. Which mountain range is divided into the Sambhar–Sirohi range and the Sambhar–Khetri range?
   a. Aravalli
   b. Satpura
   c. Himalayas

7. With which embroidery would you associate 'Tota Bagh', 'Bawan Bagh' and 'Ashrafi Bagh'?
   a. Kantha
   b. Chikankari
   c. Phulkari

8. Kamban, Krittibas and Tulsidas have all written different versions of which work?
   a. Ramayana
   b. Vedas
   c. Mahabharata

9. Who served as the prime minister of India for about seventeen years?
   a. Jawaharlal Nehru
   b. Indira Gandhi
   c. P.V. Narasimha Rao

10. Who directed the 2005 film *Iqbal*?
    a. Nagesh Kukunoor

b. Mohit Suri
c. Meera Nair

WHAT'S THE QUESTION

1. It was the first month of the early Roman calendar.
2. It comprised one big Oscar and seven little ones.
3. The fabric calico is named after a city in this state of India.
4. In the Ramayana, he was Shatrughna's father.
5. He wrote *Our Trees Still Grow in Dehra*.
6. Nadir Shah gave its name
7. *Moonwalk* (book)
8. Changi Airport
9. Kyats
10. William the Conqueror defeated King Harold II of England

MIXED BAG

1. In 1930, who started the Vanar Sena, a children's brigade to help freedom fighters?
2. It is one of the largest Indian antelopes. The male of the species has a smooth bluish-grey coat and is also called 'blue bull'. How is it commonly known in India?
3. Which Indian emulated Bob Massie's feat of sixteen wickets on Test debut?
4. What would you associate with 'going under the hammer'?
5. Which historically important structure of the Mughals is also known as 'Fort Rouge' or 'Qila-i-Akbari'?

6. Which term, also meaning 'to fix firmly and deeply in a surrounding mass', was used to describe journalists who travelled with allied army formations during the Gulf War of 2003?

7. The Bronx, Brooklyn, Queens, Staten Island and Manhattan together form which city?

8. If you had excess bilirubin in your bloodstream, what would you be suffering from?

9. Name the American president and his wife who acted in the 1957 film Hellcats of the Navy.

10. Which Mughal emperor planted 1,00,000 mango trees in Darbhanga, Bihar at a place now known as Lakhi Bagh?

SPOT THE ANSWER

1. Who had four sons named Harilal, Manilal, Ramdas and Devdas?
   a. Subhas Chandra Bose
   b. Bhagat Singh
   c. Mahatma Gandhi

2. The Danjon scale, ranging from L=0 (meaning very dark) to L=4 (meaning very bright copper red to orange), measures the brightness of which phenomenon?
   a. Lunar eclipse
   b. Aurora Borealis
   c. Rainbow

3. In Japan, what would you do with a kimono?

    a. Wear it

    b. Eat it

    c. Write with it

4. Noshak is the highest point of which country?
   a. Pakistan
   b. China
   c. Afghanistan

5. How did espresso coffee get its name?
   a. A variation of the word 'express'
   b. From the word 'espressino', meaning cold coffee
   c. From the Italian word for 'pressed out'

CONFIDENCE ROUND

1. Which famous astrologer was born in 1503 and died in 1566?
2. In Hinduism, swarg is heaven or hell?
3. Some owls are also active during the day: serious or joking?
4. Complete the title of this Hindi film: *Jo Jeeta Wohi_____*
5. What is the shape of the balls used in the Adelaide Oval?
6. In the works by Agatha Christie, what was Miss Marple's first name?
7. Mg is the symbol of which chemical element: manganese or magnesium?
8. Which of these rivers flows through the states of Karnataka and Tamil Nadu: Cauvery or Narmada?

9. Which fruit, rich in papain, an enzyme present in its milky juice, is normally used to make meat tender?
10. A pentathlon has five, ten or fifteen events?

WHAT'S THE WORD

Set 1

1. Who is the first Indian woman to scale the summit of Mount Everest?
2. In which Indian state is the Manas Wildlife Sanctuary?
3. Which Indian said, 'Wars cannot be won by bullets, but only by bleeding hearts'?
4. Which was Anna Sewell's only published novel?
5. What is defined in the dictionary as 'a report, especially in a newspaper, which gives the news of someone's death and details about their life'?
6. How many fish would you have if you had one cod, three jellyfish and four crayfish?
7. What's the word?

Set 2

1. Which emperor was the great grandfather of Aurangzeb?
2. Which Indian state was previously called the United Provinces?
3. What colour does blue litmus paper turn into when put in acid?
4. Which novel by Charles Dickens is subtitled *The Parish Boy's Progress*?
5. Which narrow bones form the cage around your heart and lungs?

6. In the place of which common word would you use an ampersand?
7. What's the word?

Set 3

1. Cirrus, cirrocumulus, stratus and nimbostratus are types of what?
2. What is the name of the first Asterix book?
3. Which musical instrument was referred to as Shata-Tantri Veena in ancient times?
4. According to mythology, who lifted the Govardhana mountain?
5. Think logically! Which planet was the first to be explored by man?
6. What don't manx cats and humans have, that most monkeys do?
7. What's the word?

Set 4

1. Barking, swamp, musk and rein are all types of which animal?
2. The leaves of which tree appear on the flag of the United Nations?
3. Which word meaning a short official note, memorandum, or voucher, typically recording a sum owed comes from a Hindi word meaning 'note, pass'?
4. Which sport was originally known as *jeu de paumme* in French meaning the game of the palm?
5. Which city in the United Kingdom is known as the 'City of Spires' for its Gothic towers and steeples:

Glasgow or Oxford?

6. *Oryza sativa* is the scientific name of which food grain?
7. What's the word?

Set 5

1. Which Mughal emperor was born at Umarkot in 1542?
2. Name the largest species of rat found in India. (Hint: In Telugu, it is called *pandi-kokku*.)
3. Popeye has an anchor tattooed on his arm. What tattoo do his four nephews have?
4. In India, which embroidery uses white yarn on colourless muslins called *tanzeb*?
5. Which planet was discovered by astronomer William Herschel?
6. Of which music group are Pakistan-based Bilal Maqsood and Faisal Kapadia members?
7. What's the word?

MATHS AND IQ

1. How is my father's only sister's paternal grandfather's only grandson related to me?
2. Fill in the blanks with either addition, subtraction, multiplication or division to figure out the correct answer. Go sequentially from left to right without following BODMAS.

23		14		15		2	=	11

3. In a certain code, if MONITOR is written as OMPGVMT, how is CURSOR written?
4. Which number will logically complete the sequence?

7, 12, 22, 37, 57, ____

5. Fill in the blanks with either addition, subtraction, multiplication or division to figure out the correct answer. Go sequentially from left to right without following BODMAS.

43		10		3		2	=	13

VOCABULARY

1. Rearrange the letters of the word 'DEAR' to get what you do when you open a book.
2. Rearrange the letters of the word 'PLANE' to get an Asian country.
3. Rearrange the letters of the word 'LEAK' to get a water body.
4. Read the word 'LAGER' backwards to get a word meaning 'royal'.
5. Read the word 'BAT' backwards to get a computer key or small flap.

SPEED

1. Which story by Louisa May Alcott is about four sisters: Meg, Jo, Beth and Amy?
2. In World War II, what was the US's M-4 General Sherman?
3. On which part of the body are mittens worn?
4. Over 70 per cent of the population of greater one-horned rhinos occurs in which national park?
5. Think differently! Which part of a mechanical watch sounds like it had a previous owner?

6. Nippon or Nihon is another name for which country?
7. What makes up 99.8 per cent of the mass of the entire solar system?
8. Who became the president of Argentina after the death of Juan Perón in 1974?
9. In Chinese, the name of which food item literally means 'stir-fried' noodles?
10. On which famous street is the New York Stock Exchange located?

ANSWERS

TAKE YOUR PICK

1. Madri
2. Gold
3. Taj Mahal
4. The International Committee of the Red Cross
5. Parsis
6. Aravalli
7. Phulkari
8. Ramayana
9. Jawaharlal Nehru
10. Nagesh Kukunoor

WHAT'S THE QUESTION

1. What is March?
2. What was unusual about the Oscar presented to Walt Disney for *Snow White and the Seven Dwarfs*?
3. What is Kerala?
4. Who was Dasharatha?
5. Name a book by Ruskin Bond.
6. Who gave the Koh-i-noor diamond its name?
7. What is the title of Michael Jackson's autobiography?
8. What is the name of Singapore's airport?
9. What is the currency of Myanmar (formerly Burma)?
10. Who defeated who at the Battle of Hastings (1066 CE)?

MIXED BAG

1. Indira Gandhi
2. Nilgai
3. Narendra Hirwani
4. Going to be sold at an auction
5. Agra Fort
6. Embed
7. New York City
8. Jaundice
9. Ronald and Nancy Reagan
10. Akbar

SPOT THE ANSWER

1. Mahatma Gandhi
2. Lunar eclipse
3. Wear it
4. Afghanistan
5. From the Italian word for 'pressed out'

CONFIDENCE ROUND

1. Nostradamus
2. Heaven
3. Serious
4. *Sikander*
5. Round
6. Jane
7. Magnesium
8. Cauvery

9. Papaya
10. Five

WHAT'S THE WORD

Set 1

1. Bachendri Pal
2. Assam
3. Mahatma Gandhi
4. *Black Beauty*
5. Obituary
6. One. Cod is a fish. Jellyfish and crayfish are not fish.
7. BAMBOO

Set 2

1. Akbar
2. Uttar Pradesh
3. Red
4. *Oliver Twist*
5. Ribs
6. And
7. AURORA

Set 3

1. Clouds
2. *Asterix the Gaul*
3. Santoor
4. Krishna
5. Earth
6. Tails
7. CASKET

Set 4

1. Deer
2. Olive
3. Chit
4. Tennis
5. Oxford
6. Rice
7. DOCTOR

Set 5

1. Akbar
2. Bandicoot
3. Anchors as well
4. *Chikankari*
5. Uranus
6. Strings
7. ABACUS

MATHS AND IQ

1. My father

2.

23	Plus	14	Minus	15	Divided	2	=	11

3. ESTQQP

4. 82 (7+5=12, 12+10=22, 22+15=37, 37+20=57, 57+25=82)

5.

43	Minus	10	Divided	3	Plus	2	=	13

VOCABULARY

1. READ

2. NEPAL
3. LAKE
4. REGAL
5. TAB

SPEED

1. *Little Women*
2. A tank
3. Hands
4. Kaziranga National Park
5. The second hand
6. Japan
7. The sun
8. Isabel Perón
9. Chow Mein
10. Wall Street

SET 12

TAKE YOUR PICK

1. Who became Uttara's dance and music teacher at Raja Virata's court?
   a. Arjuna
   b. Bhima
   c. Sahadeva

2. The name of which shiny mineral means 'crumb' in Latin?
   a. Silver
   b. Mica
   c. Platinum

3. Which of these was the principal seat of authority of the Chandela rulers?
   a. Khajuraho
   b. Mahabalipuram
   c. Hampi

4. Which of these spices is produced by treating the crimson stigma of a flower?
   a. Mace
   b. Turmeric
   c. Saffron

5. In his travelogue, which island did Marco Polo refer to as the 'Female Island'?
   a. Minicoy
   b. Little Andaman
   c. Great Nicobar

6. In the abbreviation ATM, what does 'M' stand for?
   a. Machine
   b. Mobile
   c. Money

7. Who invited Atomba Singh to teach Manipuri dancing in Bengal in the 1920s?
   a. Mahatma Gandhi
   b. Rabindranath Tagore
   c. Subhas Chandra Bose

8. In 2002, a dinosaur was named in honour of which famous science fiction author?
   a. Arthur C. Clarke
   b. Stephen King
   c. Michael Crichton

9. From 1977 to 1979, Atal Bihari Vajpayee was Union cabinet minister of…
   a. Information and Broadcasting
   b. External Affairs
   c. Civil Aviation

10. In 1896, what took place for the first time in India at Watson's Hotel in Mumbai?

a. First Congress annual session
b. First film screening
c. First Filmfare Awards

WHAT'S THE QUESTION

1. JFK International Airport
2. Florence Nightingale played an important role in this war from 1853-1856.
3. *Pride and Prejudice* is one of her most famous novels.
4. Ringgit
5. Taming the ferocious horses of Diomedes and overcoming the Nemaean lion.
6. They are the only mammal capable of true flight.
7. He married Dimple Kapadia in 1973.
8. In *Asterix* comics, he fell into a cauldron of magic potion when he was a little boy.
9. Ophiuchus
10. She is Lava and Kusha's mother.

MIXED BAG

1. Tanzania was formed by the merger of which two sovereign states?
2. Sarojini Naidu was the governor of UP. Name her daughter, who became the governor of West Bengal.
3. A species of which member of the weasel family is called 'fisi maji,' meaning water hyena in Swahili?
4. Traditionally, which famous sporting event is associated with strawberries and cream?
5. Robert Clive fought Siraj-ud-Daula in the Battle of

Plassey in 1757. In which present-day Indian state is Plassey located?

6. Which word connects the repetition of sound caused by the reflection of sound waves and a code word representing the letter E, used in radio communication?

7. Which is the senior-most regiment in the Indian Army?

8. I am a nine-letter word. My first letter is the Roman letter for 100. The next three are a zodiac sign and the last two are the name of the Egyptian Sun God. Who am I?

9. Name the antibiotic also known as the first 'wonder drug'.

10. Which crime fighter's parents were killed by Joe 'Chill' Chilton?

SPOT THE ANSWER

1. With reference to the World Wide Web, what does the term 'hit rate' refer to?
   a. Cricket scores on the net
   b. Being hit by a virus
   c. The number of visitors to a website

2. In Hindi films, Begum Mumtaz Jehan Dehlavi was the original name of which actress?
   a. Madhubala
   b. Meena Kumari
   c. Waheeda Rahman

3. In 2006, which country slapped a 5 per cent tax on chopsticks over concerns of deforestation?
   a. Egypt
   b. Korea
   c. China

4. Why do bees perform a complicated movement called the 'waggle dance'?
   a. To teach young bees to fly
   b. To tell other bees where to find food
   c. To warn bees from other hives

5. Who sang 'The Song for Peace' minutes before he was assassinated?
   a. John F. Kennedy
   b. Abraham Lincoln
   c. Yitzhak Rabin

CONFIDENCE ROUND

1. Which Italian city has a famous leaning tower?
2. Which scientist coined the name 'oxygen'?
3. Which term relates to horses: equine or porcine?
4. The Nag river flows by Nagpur: serious or joking?
5. Shah Shuja and Aurangzeb were the sons of which Mughal emperor: Shah Jahan or Jahangir?
6. In comics, Popeye and Brutus compete with each other for whose affection?
7. The Ranji Trophy was named after which former cricketer?
8. What would a Chinese individual do with a won ton?

9. How is Rahul Gandhi related to Feroze Varun Gandhi?
10. What does 'I' in FBI stand for: Intelligence or Investigation?

WHAT'S THE WORD

Set 1

1. Which vehicle was originally a mobile temporary hospital that followed the army from place to place?
2. Which of these is often called the unicorns of the sea: Narwhal or Beluga?
3. What is nearly equal to 2.54 cm: an inch or a foot?
4. After which famous historical leader is the capital of Gujarat named?
5. Spanning seven countries, which is the longest continental mountain range in the world?
6. The name of which popular board game for two to four players comes from the Latin word meaning 'I play'?
7. What's the word?

Set 2

1. Siamese, Persian, Caffre and Sphynx are all types of which animal?
2. Which unit of weight is one-sixteenth of a pound: gram or ounce?
3. In India, which monument is seen on the reverse side of the ₹50 note?
4. Red is a primary colour or a secondary colour?
5. In which continent is Spain located?

6. On a Scrabble board, the score for an entire word is tripled when one of its letters is placed on a square of which colour?
7. What's the word?

Set 3

1. Name the Chinese pilgrim who came to India during the reign of Chandragupta II.
2. What are Basmati and Manipuri different varieties of: roti or rice?
3. Other than India, which Asian country begins with the letters 'Ind' and ends with 'ia'?
4. Which caves have been excavated out of the vertical face of Charanandri Hills?
5. The inability of which gas to support life led Antoine-Laurent Lavoisier to name it 'azote'?
6. Name the most well-known extinct flightless bird of Mauritius.
7. What's the word?

Set 4

1. What is the colour of emerald?
2. Muhi-al-Din Muhammad was the original name of which great Mughal emperor?
3. Which lake in India shares its name with the Hindi name of pulses?
4. If 'Big Bird' is the nickname for cricketer Joel Garner, then which footballer was nicknamed the 'Little Bird'?
5. Which Greek nymph's hopeless love for Narcissus made her fade away until only her voice remained?
6. Who was raised by the apes: Mowgli or Tarzan?

7. What's the word?

Set 5

1. Which of these is an amphibian: frog or turtle?
2. In the world of music, what would you associate with Shellac, Vulcanite, Columbia, Edison Diamond and Vinyl?
3. In India, if a woman can vote at the age of eighteen, at what minimum age can a man vote?
4. Is Ooty in the Nilgiris or Aravallis?
5. The Latin name for which metal is *cuprum*?
6. In India, how is a flag flown when there is a state mourning: full mast or half mast?
7. What's the word?

MATHS AND IQ

1. In a class, Indumati's rank is 12th from the top and 32nd from the bottom. How many students are there in the class?
2. Fill in the blanks with either addition, subtraction, multiplication or division to figure out the correct answer. Go sequentially from left to right without following BODMAS.

25		3		16		7	=	13

3. Which set of letters will logically follow the pattern ZIFZY, IFZYZ, FZYZI, _____
4. Fill in the blanks with either addition, subtraction, multiplication or division to figure out the correct answer. Go sequentially from left to right without following BODMAS.

7		4		27		5	=	11

5. If you add all the dots on a dice, except 4, which number would you get?

VOCABULARY

1. Rearrange the letters of the word 'LATE' to get a word that means story.
2. Rearrange the letters of the word 'SAVE' to get an object you might put flowers in.
3. Rearrange the letters of the word 'LEAST' to get a word that means 'to take something illegally or without permission'.
4. Read the word 'PART' backwards to get a device to catch animals.
5. Read the word 'LIAR' backwards to get what trains run on.

SPEED

1. In 1325, Prince Jauna became ruler under which name?
2. What constitutes more than 50 per cent of a dried date, in terms of weight?
3. Which is the only even prime number?
4. Which organ in the human body is the word 'pulmonary' connected with?
5. In which sport were Misha Grewal and Bhuvaneshwari Kumari women's national champions?
6. A camel's stomach is divided into how many chambers?

7. Who was the first Indian to receive both the Nobel Prize and the Bharat Ratna?
8. Which desert covers almost all of Botswana?
9. Which musical instrument is also known as venu, vamsi, murali, pillankarovi and kolalu?
10. Which planet was named by the Romans after their god of war because of its red, blood-like colour?

ANSWERS

TAKE YOUR PICK

1. Arjuna
2. Mica
3. Khajuraho. It is a village in Madhya Pradesh.
4. Saffron
5. Minicoy
6. Machine (ATM = Automated Teller Machine)
7. Rabindranath Tagore
8. Michael Crichton
9. External Affairs
10. First film screening

WHAT'S THE QUESTION

1. What was the Idlewild Airport renamed as in 1963?
2. What is the Crimean War?
3. Who is Jane Austen?
4. What is the currency of Malaysia?
5. Name any two of Hercules' Twelve Labours.
6. What are bats?
7. Who was Rajesh Khanna?
8. Who is Obelix?
9. What is sometimes called the thirteenth sign of the zodiac?
10. Who is Sita?

MIXED BAG
1. Tanganyika and Zanzibar
2. Padmaja Naidu
3. Otter
4. Wimbledon Tennis Championships
5. West Bengal
6. Echo
7. The president's bodyguard
8. Cleopatra
9. Penicillin
10. Bruce Wayne/Batman

SPOT THE ANSWER

1. The number of visitors to a website
2. Madhubala
3. China
4. To tell other bees where to find food
5. Yitzhak Rabin. He was the prime minister of Israel, and led peace negotiations with Palestine and neighbouring Arab countries.

CONFIDENCE ROUND

1. Pisa
2. Antoine Lavoisier
3. Equine
4. Serious
5. Shah Jahan
6. Olive Oyl
7. K.S. Ranjitsinhji (1872–1933), who played Test cricket

for England.
8. Eat it or cook it
9. They are cousins.
10. Investigation

WHAT'S THE WORD

Set 1

1. Ambulance
2. Narwhal
3. Inch
4. Mahatma Gandhi
5. Andes
6. Ludo
7. ANIMAL

Set 2

1. Cat
2. Ounce
3. Parliament of India
4. Primary colour
5. Europe
6. Red
7. COPPER

Set 3

1. Fa-hien
2. Rice
3. Indonesia
4. Ellora Caves
5. Nitrogen

6. Dodo
7. FRIEND

Set 4

1. Green
2. Aurangazeb
3. Dal Lake
4. Garrincha
5. Echo
6. Tarzan
7. GADGET

Set 5

1. Frog
2. Records (LPs)
3. Eighteen
4. Nilgiris
5. Copper
6. Half mast
7. FRENCH

MATHS AND IQ

1. 43 (12+31)

2.

25	Multiply	3	Plus	16	Divide	7	=	13

3. ZYZIF

4.

7	Multiply	4	Plus	27	Divide	5	=	11

5. 17

VOCABULARY

1. TALE
2. VASE
3. STEAL
4. TRAP
5. RAIL

SPEED

1. Muhammad bin Tughluq
2. Sugar
3. 2
4. The lungs
5. Squash
6. Three
7. C. V. Raman
8. Kalahari
9. Flute
10. Mars

SET 13

TAKE YOUR PICK

1. In the Mahabharata, Duryodhana cried like which creature when he was born?
   a. Ass
   b. Horse
   c. Elephant

2. Which equation does David Bodanis call 'the world's most famous equation' in a biography of the equation?
   a. pr^2
   b. $E=mc^2$
   c. sxt

3. Which leader said 'Every blow aimed at me is a nail in the coffin of British imperialism'?
   a. Lal Bahadur Shastri
   b. Lala Lajpat Rai
   c. Bipin Chandra Pal

4. The roads of which Indian Union Territory were based on a unique plan called 7Vs by its original planner?
   a. Puducherry
   b. Andaman and Nicobar Islands
   c. Chandigarh

5. The name of which popular flavour comes from the Spanish word for 'pod'?
   a. Vanilla
   b. Strawberry
   c. Orange

6. What is the surname of Parvati in the *Harry Potter* series of books?
   a. Patil
   b. Peter
   c. Sarawati

7. Who is the author of *Natyashastra*?
   a. Bhasa
   b. Tulsidas
   c. Bharata Muni

8. Which Nobel Laureate's autobiography is *Freedom in Exile*?
   a. Nelson Mandela
   b. Dalai Lama
   c. Aung San Suu Kyi

9. What fraction of the Rajya Sabha retires every second year?
   a. Half
   b. One-third
   c. One-fourth

10. In a famous song from the film *Shree 420*, which accessory does Raj Kapoor describe as 'Roosi'?

a. Patloon
b. Topi
c. Joota

WHAT'S THE QUESTION

1. He was appointed editor of the newspaper, *Avanti!* in 1912.
2. They were a race of one-eyed giants; one of them was Polyphemus.
3. *Goal*
4. Bram Stoker
5. UN Day
6. The only country to have an actual building on its national flag.
7. Spirit of St Louis
8. It is a word puzzle with a grid of squares and blanks.
9. 10 Downing Street
10. Nephrons are the functional units of this organ.

MIXED BAG

1. Which is the largest country in Central America, with a coastline on both the Atlantic and the Pacific Ocean?
2. Who was the first Chairman of the Rajya Sabha?
3. Only one forest is the home of the Asiatic lion. Name it.
4. Which cricketer's autobiography is titled *Beyond 10,000, My Life Story*?
5. Which famous mausoleum was called 'a teardrop on

the cheek of time' by Rabindranath Tagore?

6. Who was issued India's first pilot's licence in 1929?

7. Who was the first National Professor of independent India?

8. Which was the first country to gain independence in the new millennium (2001–02)?

9. Who was awarded the Nobel Prize 'because of his profoundly sensitive, fresh and beautiful verse, by which, with consummate skill, he has made his poetic thought, expressed in his own English words, a part of the literature of the West'?

10. Which 1992 animated film had the tagline 'Imagine if you had three wishes, three hopes, three dreams and they all could come true'?

SPOT THE ANSWER

1. What is a plectrum used for?
   a. To strum a stringed instrument
   b. To break light into various colours
   c. To safeguard electrical appliances

2. Which cartoon character is called 'Skipper Skræk' in Denmark?
   a. Tintin
   b. Asterix
   c. Popeye

3. In medieval times, a knight threw down a gauntlet to challenge someone to a duel. Which part of his attire did a gauntlet refer to?

    a. The plume from his helmet
    b. His gloves
    c. His broadsword

4. Lexico was the original name for which board game?
    a. Snakes and ladders
    b. Scrabble
    c. Monopoly

5. The word 'solstice' comes from the Latin phrase meaning...
    a. A salt cellar
    b. A five-pointed star
    c. Sun stands still

CONFIDENCE ROUND

1. A chipmunk is a squirrel or a rabbit?
2. Which of these hill stations is located in Tamil Nadu: Ooty or Nainital?
3. What is the plural of Governor-General?
4. In 2001, which Australian became the youngest man to be ranked world number one in tennis?
5. The name of which Shah Rukh Khan starrer is shortened as *DDLJ*?
6. What kind of an animal was Black Beauty in the book of the same name?
7. Generally, how many wheels does a cycle rickshaw have?
8. What is Lord Krishna's panchajanya: conch shell or mace?

9. If a small circle has 360 degrees, how many degrees does a big circle have?

10. Which ruler died while leading his troops on the battlefield: Tipu Sultan or Humayun?

WHAT'S THE WORD

Set 1

1. Whose autobiography is called *The Fairy Tale of My Life*?
2. Which Pandava was also known as Dhananjaya?
3. Which is a flattened Indian bread: kalakand or naan?
4. Which cartoon character has nephews named Huey, Dewey and Louie?
5. Which Indian prime minister was born near Varanasi but died in the capital of Uzbekistan?
6. On a computer keyboard, what does 'Esc' stand for?
7. What's the word?

Set 2

1. Which book was written by Jayadeva: *Gita Govinda* or *Sur Sagar*?
2. *Olea europaea* is the scientific name of which tree?
3. In which country would you be if you spent takas?
4. Kargil is located in which Lok Sabha constituency?
5. Which channel is known as *La Manche* in French: English Channel or Dominica Channel?
6. Who is also known as the 'Tiger of Mysore'?
7. What's the word?

Set 3

1. Which month in the Gregorian calendar is named after Julius Caesar?
2. Who has served as the chief minister of Madhya Pradesh: Rabri Devi or Uma Bharti?
3. Triton is the largest satellite of which planet?
4. Panaji is the capital of which state of India?
5. The largest variety of which creature is the Komodo Dragon?
6. The Euro symbol is inspired by which Greek letter?
7. What's the word?

Set 4

1. Which state shares a border with Jharkhand: Bihar or Haryana?
2. Which actor is sometimes referred to as Khiladi Kumar?
3. Which famous South African leader is popularly known as Madiba?
4. In terms of average elevation, which is the highest continent in the world?
5. In war parlance, which three words do you use for the stretch of ground between two enemy lines?
6. Limba Ram represented India in which sport?
7. What's the word?

Set 5

1. What would a Scotsman do with a kilt: eat it or wear it?
2. Which Greek goddess shares her name with a part of the eye?
3. Which sport did Douglas Jardine play for England?

4. Which actress is married to Ajay Devgn?
5. What would you call the official residence of an ambassador?
6. Which card is used to predict one's future: tarot card or flash card?
7. What's the word?

MATHS AND IQ

1. OBMHNMHO : PANGOLIN :: SPQUNJRF : ?
2. Fill in the blanks with either addition, subtraction, multiplication or division to figure out the correct answer. Go sequentially from left to right without following BODMAS.

19		3		14		67	=	4

3. Nalini's total bill at a restaurant was ₹84, including the waiter's tip of 5 per cent. What was the bill amount excluding the waiter's tip?
4. Joy is taller than Rishi but shorter than Rinku. Rahul is taller than Manisha but shorter than Rishi. Who is the shortest of them all?
5. Fill in the blanks with either addition, subtraction, multiplication or division to figure out the correct answer. Go sequentially from left to right without following BODMAS.

38		14		21		5	=	9

VOCABULARY

1. Rearrange the letters of the word 'NONE' to get a

colourless gas.

2. Rearrange the letters of the word 'TIMER' to get a level of excellence.

3. Rearrange the letters of the word 'AGES' to get a religious person.

4. Read the word 'DRAW' backwards to get a room in a hospital.

5. Read the word 'AVID' backward to mean a female opera singer.

SPEED

1. Which rodent gives its name to a device attached to a computer?

2. Which war ended at 11 a.m. on the eleventh day of the eleventh month in 1918?

3. What milk-based product is the main ingredient of shrikhand?

4. What important part did James Phipps play in the history of medicine?

5. Which Pandava was also known as Dharmaputra?

6. Little Miss Muffet was afraid of spiders: serious or joking?

7. How many hands does an ambidextrous man have?

8. Is the Krishna river mainly in Andhra Pradesh or Tamil Nadu?

9. Who was Kareena Kapoor's grandfather?

10. With which art form is Anjolie Ela Menon associated?

ANSWERS

TAKE YOUR PICK

1. Ass
2. $E = mc^2$
3. Lala Lajpat Rai
4. Chandigarh
5. Vanilla (The flavouring essence is derived from the pods of the vanilla orchid.)
6. Patil
7. Bharata Muni
8. Dalai Lama
9. One-third
10. Topi. The song was sung by Mukesh.

WHAT'S THE QUESTION

1. Who was Benito Mussolini?
2. Who were the Cyclopes? (singular: Cyclops)
3. Name Dhyan Chand's autobiography.
4. Who wrote *Dracula*?
5. What is 24 October celebrated as?
6. What is unique about the flag of Cambodia?
7. What was the name of Charles Lindbergh's aircraft in which he made the first solo transatlantic flight?
8. What is a crossword?
9. What is the address of the official office and residence of the prime minister of the United Kingdom?

10. What is kidney?

MIXED BAG

1. Nicaragua
2. Dr S. Radhakrishnan
3. Gir Forest in Gujarat
4. Allan Border
5. Taj Mahal
6. J.R.D. Tata
7. C. V. Raman
8. East Timor
9. Rabindranath Tagore
10. *Aladdin*

SPOT THE ANSWER

1. To strum a stringed instrument. It is a small bit of teardrop-shaped or triangular plastic.
2. Popeye
3. His gloves
4. Scrabble
5. Sun stands still

CONFIDENCE ROUND

1. Squirrel
2. Ooty
3. Governors-General
4. Lleyton Hewitt (Twenty years old)
5. *Dilwale Dulhania Le Jayenge*

6. Horse
7. Three
8. Conch shell
9. 360
10. Tipu Sultan

WHAT'S THE WORD

Set 1

1. Hans Christian Andersen
2. Arjuna
3. Naan
4. Donald Duck
5. Lal Bahadur Shastri
6. Escape
7. HANDLE

Set 2

1. *Gita Govinda*
2. Olive
3. Bangladesh
4. Ladakh
5. English Channel
6. Tipu Sultan
7. GOBLET

Set 3

1. July
2. Uma Bharti
3. Neptune
4. Goa

5. Lizard
6. Epsilon
7. JUNGLE

Set 4

1. Bihar
2. Akshay Kumar
3. Nelson Mandela
4. Antarctica
5. No man's land
6. Archery
7. BANANA

Set 5

1. Wear it
2. Iris
3. Cricket
4. Kajol
5. Embassy
6. Tarot card
7. WICKET

MATHS AND IQ

1. TORTOISE
2.

19	Multiply	3	Plus	14	Minus	67	=	4

3. ₹80
4. Manisha
5.

38	Minus	14	Plus	21	Divide	5	=	9

VOCABULARY

1. NEON
2. MERIT
3. SAGE
4. WARD
5. DIVA

SPEED

1. Mouse
2. World War I
3. Yoghurt/Curd
4. He was the boy who was given the first vaccination against smallpox by Edward Jenner.
5. Yudhisthir
6. Serious
7. Two
8. Andhra Pradesh
9. Raj Kapoor
10. Painting

TAKE YOUR PICK

1. According to Hindu mythology, who is the king of the yakshas?
   a. Kubera
   b. Skanda
   c. Yama

2. Which battle of Panipat was fought in the eighteenth century?
   a. First
   b. Second
   c. Third

3. What do Adelie penguins use to mark their nests?
   a. Pebbles
   b. Fish
   c. Feathers

4. The name of which food item comes from French words meaning 'baked twice'?
   a. Pizza
   b. Biscuit
   c. Cake

5. Which island of New York has four counties: Kings,

Queens, Nassau and Suffolk?
a. Long Island
b. Loyalty Islands
c. Falkland Islands

6. Which of these novels was written by Vikram Seth in verse?
a. *The Glass Palace*
b. *The God of Small Things*
c. *The Golden Gate*

7. In the eighteenth century, which metal did King Louis XV of France declare as the only metal fit for a king?
a. Platinum
b. Silver
c. Iron

8. Which Indian musician's father was the diwan of the Maharaja of Jhalawar?
a. Pandit Ravi Shankar
b. Ustad Zakir Hussain
c. Pandit Shiv Kumar Sharma

9. If the colour of your school sweater is carmine, which colour is it?
a. Deep red
b. Deep blue
c. Reddish-green

10. Which prime minister of India was around three years old when India became independent?

    a. V.P. Singh
    b. Rajiv Gandhi
    c. I.K. Gujral

WHAT'S THE QUESTION

1. It was Ian Fleming's only children's story.
2. Jacob Schick
3. It is a deadly disease caused by a bacteria, *Yersinia pestis*.
4. Kill Devil Hills
5. The Kauravas and Pandavas fought their great war here.
6. This fish is also known as 'caribe'.
7. His name is Kvack.
8. In 1862, he proposed the formation of voluntary relief societies in his book *A Memory of Solferino*.
9. He wrote *Indica*.
10. Emperor, Gentoo, Galapagos

MIXED BAG

1. On which African river is the Victoria Falls located?
2. Who was the only Indian Governor-General of independent India?
3. Which North American animal is referred to as the 'Silvertip Bear' because the tips of the hair on its body is silver-coloured?
4. Harsh Mankad represented India in the Davis Cup. In which sport did his father, Ashok Mankad, represent India?

5. Which Indian city did Job Charnock 'find' in 1690?
6. What is a gentleman's agreement?
7. What does a car's radiator do?
8. Which famous book by Charles Dickens ends with the line: 'God bless us, everyone!'?
9. If you were visiting the archaeological areas of Pompeii, Herculaneum and Torre Annunziata, which country would you be in?
10. Who is the first actor to receive three consecutive Filmfare Awards in the Best Actor category?

SPOT THE ANSWER

1. The word simian is used to describe what?
   a. Sheep
   b. Snakes
   c. Monkeys

2. Hidrosis is the medical term for...
   a. Water in the brain
   b. Death due to drowning
   c. Perspiration

3. Which soccer star's reluctance to board a plane earned him the nickname 'The non-flying Dutchman'?
   a. Diego Maradona
   b. Eric Cantona
   c. Dennis Bergkamp

4. How is nyctalopia better known?
   a. Blindness

    b. Conjunctivitis

    c. Night blindness

5. What would the term 'Round Robin' best describe?
   a. A bird's nest
   b. A tournament in which each competitor plays in turn against every other
   c. A steamed pudding

CONFIDENCE ROUND

1. What would you call an ice cream that has fruits in it: candy or tutti-frutti?
2. Which is used to measure depth: a fathom or a farad?
3. What was held at Rajagriha, Vaishali, Pataliputra and Kundalavahana: Buddhist councils or appointment of Khalsa?
4. Which state is larger in area: Chhattisgarh or Madhya Pradesh?
5. How many sleeves do thirty white shirts have?
6. Which country's ancient emperors held the title Mikado?
7. In cricket, which continent has the most number of Test-playing nations?
8. What is the present name of the city where Aung San Suu Kyi was born?
9. A drake is a male horse: serious or joking?
10. What term is used to describe words or drawing scribbled on a wall: graffiti or cartoon?

WHAT'S THE WORD

Set 1

1. Which George was the first president of USA: Washington or Orwell?
2. *Electrophorus electricus* is the scientific name of which fish?
3. In Latin, what means forefinger: index or preface?
4. Alaknanda and Bhagirathi are the two main headstreams of which river?
5. Which part of Achilles' body was vulnerable (his weak point)?
6. Akhenaten was the father of which famous boy king?
7. What's the word?

Set 2

1. A high plateau named Lakshmi Planum is located on which planet?
2. The ancient Egyptians regarded the spherical bulb of which vegetable as a symbol of the universe?
3. In Yahoo.com, what does 'Y' in Yahoo stand for?
4. In *The Merchant of Venice*, from whom did Shylock wish to take his pound of flesh?
5. How do we know the rhizome of the plant *Zingiber officinale*?
9. Michael Vaughan captained which team in Test cricket?
7. What's the word?

Set 3

1. By what name is the Baha'i Temple in New Delhi

popularly known?
2. Which word is used to describe signatures given by celebrities to their fans?
3. The Sundarbans is situated in a valley or a delta?
4. What is the common name for a form of *seborrheic dermatitis* that affects the scalp?
5. What is the North American term for lift: elevator or subway?
6. If RAM stands for Random Access Memory, what does ROM stand for?
7. What's the word?

Set 4

1. Pushkar is famous for its camel fair. What is Etawah famous for?
2. Which Mughal emperor founded the city Allahabad?
3. Which country did Indira Gandhi call 'Chhota Bharat'?
4. If the letter 'T' in ET stands for terrestrial, what does the letter 'E' stand for?
5. Which event is celebrated in the first month of the Gregorian calendar: Republic Day or Independence Day?
6. According to legend, Newton discovered gravity after what fell on his head?
7. What's the word?

Set 5

1. A rabbit's tail is called a scut. What is a fox's tail called?
2. What is Udhagamandalam better known as: Ooty or Udaygiri?

3. Billie Jean King was professionally associated with which sport?
4. Which four-letter word is another name for 'making bread shorter': trim or trip?
5. Which part of the body does pneumonia mainly affect?
6. What does the 'e' in 'email' stand for?
7. What's the word?

MATHS AND IQ

1. From 2 to 49, if you add all the even multiples of 7, what will be your answer?
2. Fill in the blanks with either addition, subtraction, multiplication or division to figure out the correct answer. Go sequentially from left to right without following BODMAS.

| 18 | | 2 | | 11 | | 95 | = | 4 |

3. Rearrange the letters of the words DAINTY and COIR to get the name of a book with meaningful words.
4. How many vowels appear immediately after a consonant in the word SUPERCALIFRAGILISTICEXPIALIDOCIOUS?
5. Fill in the blanks with either addition, subtraction, multiplication or division to figure out the correct answer. Go sequentially from left to right without following BODMAS.

| 14 | | 4 | | 6 | | 10 | = | 6 |

VOCABULARY

1. Rearrange the letters of the word 'HART' to get the name of a desert.
2. Rearrange the letters of the word 'SLIP' to get a part of your face.
3. Rearrange the letters of the word 'GNU' to get a name of a weapon.
4. Read the word 'STAB' backward to get the plural of the name of a nocturnal mammal
5. Read the word 'DEER' backward to get a tall plant that grows in water

SPEED

1. Who was the last Mughal emperor of India?
2. Which prime minister of India wrote the book *The Insider*?
3. If your larynx was removed, you would suffer from which disability?
4. In 1980, the World Health Organization declared the world free of which disease?
5. What is the capital of the state of South Australia: Adelaide or Melbourne?
6. How many sides does a parallelogram have?
7. Sushmita Sen is Amartya Sen's daughter: serious or joking?
8. In 1982–83, which Indian batsman scored 1,182 runs in 11 away Test matches?
9. By what name is acetylsalicylic acid better known?
10. In nursery rhymes, what did Little Bo Peep lose?

ANSWERS

TAKE YOUR PICK

1. Kubera
2. Third. Ahmad Shah Abdali defeated the Marathas in 1761.
3. Pebbles
4. Biscuit
5. Long Island
6. *The Golden Gate*
7. Platinum
8. Pandit Ravi Shankar
9. Deep red
10. Rajiv Gandhi

WHAT'S THE QUESTION

1. What is *Chitty-Chitty-Bang-Bang*?
2. Who patented the first successfully manufactured electric razor?
3. What is plague?
4. Where did the Wright brothers' first successful flight take place?
5. What happened in Kurukshetra?
6. What is another name for Piranha?
7. In the comic strip *Hagar the Horrible*, what is the name of Hagar's family duck?

8. Who was Henri Dunant?
9. Who was Megasthenes?
10. Name three species of penguin.

MIXED BAG

1. Zambezi
2. C. Rajagopalachari
3. The grizzly bear
4. Cricket
5. Kolkata
6. An arrangement or understanding which is based upon the trust of both or all parties, rather than being legally binding.
7. It cools the engine.
8. *A Christmas Carol*
9. Italy
10. Dilip Kumar

SPOT THE ANSWER

1. Monkeys
2. Perspiration
3. Dennis Bergkamp. He played for the national football team of Netherlands, as well as for clubs like Ajax and Arsenal.
4. Night blindness
5. A tournament in which each competitor plays in turn against every other

CONFIDENCE ROUND

1. Tutti-frutti
2. Fathom
3. Buddhist Councils
4. Madhya Pradesh
5. Sixty
6. Japan
7. Asia
8. Yangon
9. Joking; it is a male duck
10. Graffiti

WHAT'S THE WORD

Set 1

1. Washington
2. Electric eel
3. Index
4. Ganges
5. His heel
6. Tutankhamen
7. WEIGHT

Set 2

1. Venus
2. Onion
3. Yet (YAHOO: Yet Another Hierarchical Officious Oracle)
4. Antonio
5. Ginger

9. England
7. VOYAGE

Set 3

1. Lotus Temple
2. Autograph
3. Delta
4. Dandruff
5. Elevator
6. Read Only Memory
7. LADDER

Set 4

1. Cattle fair
2. Akbar
3. Mauritius
4. Extra
5. Republic Day
6. An apple
7. CAMERA

Set 5

1. Brush
2. Ooty
3. Tennis
3. Trim
9. Lungs
6. Electronic
7. BOTTLE

MATHS AND IQ

1. 84
2.

18	Divided	2	Multiply	11	Minus	95	=	4

3. DICTIONARY
4. 13
5.

14	Minus	4	Multiply	6	Divided	10	=	6

VOCABULARY

1. THAR
2. LIPS
3. GUN
4. BATS
5. REED

SPEED

1. Bahadur Shah Zafar
2. P.V. Narasimha Rao
3. You would not be able to speak. The larynx is also called the 'voice box'.
4. Smallpox
5. Adelaide
6. Four
7. Joking
8. Mohinder Amarnath
9. Aspirin
10. Sheep

SET 15

TAKE YOUR PICK

1. The name of which of these means 'man of the forest' in the Malay language?
   a. Orangutan
   b. Hedgehog
   c. Jaguar

2. Who was the British prime minister when India became independent?
   a. Clement Attlee
   b. Winston Churchill
   c. Harold McMillan

3. Which water body is called *Khalije Fars* in Persian and *Bahr Fars* in Arabic?
   a. Persian Gulf
   b. Gulf of Oman
   c. Red Sea

4. Which deity rides the elephant Airavat?
   a. Indra
   b. Vishnu
   c. Shiva

5. Which famous author wrote *Euclid and His Modern*

Rivals, a rare example of a humorous work concerning mathematics?
a. Charles Dickens
b. Mark Twain
c. Lewis Carroll

6. *Time*, one of M.F. Hussain's paintings, was inspired by the poem of which famous lyricist?
a. Gulzar
b. Javed Akhtar
c. Sameer

7. If a 'boomerang' is a throwing stick, what is a 'boomslang'?
a. An African snake
b. A bouncing ball
c. A firecracker

8. Which English cricketer as well as doctor was known for treating his poorer patients without charging a fee?
a. Sir Donald Bradman
b. Viv Richards
c. W.G. Grace

9. Which Bharat Ratna awardee produced the 1990 film *Lekin*?
a. Satyajit Ray
b. M.S. Subbulakshmi
c. Lata Mangeshkar

10. Which leader was also known as 'Frontier Gandhi'?
    a. Vallabhbhai Patel
    b. Khan Abdul Ghaffar Khan
    c. Bal Gangadhar Tilak

WHAT'S THE QUESTION

1. Clementines, navels and tangerines
2. It is the hardest tissue of the human body.
3. Barbara Millicent Roberts
4. He directed *Hazaar Chaurasi Ki Maa*.
5. This space term comes from the Latin words meaning 'space' and 'sailor'.
6. Filofax
7. It is a piece of metal or plastic used to help the foot into the shoe.
8. This portable stereo cassette player with headphones was invented in 1979.
9. It is called 'loo' in north India.
10. This unit of measurement comes from 'binary' and 'digit'.

MIXED BAG

1. Which river, called *Nahr Al-Urdun* in Arabic, shares its name with an Arab country of southwest Asia?
2. Which state in India has the largest number of seats in the Lok Sabha?
3. What is North America's largest rodent?
4. The first Indian chess Grandmaster was Vishwanathan Anand. Who is the second?

5. Who erected the Tower of Victory to commemorate his victory over Mahmud Khilji of Malwa in 1440?

6. By subtracting 32, dividing by 9 and multiplying by 5, what conversion can be made?

7. What is common to Cullinan, Star of the South and Great Mogul?

8. During World War II, who offered his people only 'blood, toil, tears and sweat' as they struggled to keep their freedom?

9. Which word would describe what limericks, haikus, sonnets and ballads are?

10. Which actress won her first National Award for Best Actress for the 1974 film *Ankur*?

SPOT THE ANSWER

1. The spacecraft Clementine discovered which of these, that increases the chances that humans may some day live on the moon?
   a. A golf ball
   b. A pond of frozen ice in a crater
   c. Traces of oxygen in the moon's atmosphere

2. Which of the seven ancient wonders of the world can still be seen today?
   a. Pyramids of Giza
   b. Hanging Gardens of Babylon
   c. Pharos of Alexandria

3. Who wrote *Man-Eaters of Kumaon*?
   a. Jim Corbett

    b.   Rohinton Mistry

    c.   Ruskin Bond

4.   On what occasion did Sarojini Naidu write to Jawaharlal Nehru: 'Love to all and a kiss to the new soul of India'?

    a.   When India achieved independence

    b.   On the birth of Indira Gandhi

    c.   At the start of the Quit India Movement

5.   In *Gulliver's Travels*, what caused the war between Lilliput and Blefuscu?

    a.   Whether to break the broad or narrow end of an egg

    b.   The gold in Gulliver's ship

    c.   A land dispute

CONFIDENCE ROUND

1.   Which dynasty was founded by Hasan Gangu in 1347?

2.   In the film *The Lion King*, Simba was a lion. What kind of a creature was Timon?

3.   Lungfish really have lungs: serious or joking?

4.   Which country did gymnast Nadia Comaneci represent at the Olympics: USA or Romania?

5.   Which Shakespearean play is also known as *The Scottish Play*?

6.   If Christmas is associated with cakes, what food item is Good Friday associated with?

7.   What does a chauffeur do for a living?

8.   Which hill station is in Uttarakhand: Mussoorie or

Manali?

9. In India, how are 'cabs' mostly known?
10. Callisto and Europa are moons of Jupiter: serious or joking?

WHAT'S THE WORD

Set 1

1. Which is an Arab ship with a large triangular sail: dhow or kayak?
2. What is the colour of the disc on the National Flag of Bangladesh?
3. The Romans called which fruit *malum praecocum* or 'the apple that ripens early'?
4. Which animal was earlier called 'camelopard': giraffe or leopard?
5. If Wilbur was one of the famous Wright Brothers, who was the other?
6. In which city are the headquarters of the United Nations located?
7. What's the word?

Set 2

1. Rubric or a heading on a document was originally written in which ink: Red or Blue?
2. Which mythical animal is typically represented as a horse with a single straight horn projecting from its forehead?
3. Which insects are kept in an apiary?
4. What colour cap is awarded to English Test cricketers: blue or yellow?

5. When you inhale, does your chest expand or contract?
6. Which is the largest country in the world in terms of area?
7. What's the word?

Set 3

1. Give another name for a Mexican lion or cougar beginning with the letter 'P'.
2. Complete this trio of Indian music composers: Shankar, _____ and Loy.
3. Big Ears and Mr Plod the policeman are friends of which fictional character?
4. Who is the first Indian to claim a hat-trick in an ODI match?
5. 'Thou art the ruler of the minds' (when translated) is the opening line of the National Anthem of which country?
6. Does Brahma sit on a lotus or a rose?
7. What's the word?

Set 4

1. Which festival connects Bohag or Rongali, Kati or Kangali, and Magh or Bhogali?
2. A German submarine used in the First or Second World War was called a U-boat or a Merchant ship?
3. *Back to the Mark* is the autobiography of which former fast bowler?
4. Which Hindu god is called Vighna Harta as he removes obstacles?
5. An extremely expensive possession to keep is often referred to as 'a white _____'.

6. Name the second largest US state in terms of area. (Hint: Austin is the capital and Houston is its largest city.)
7. What's the word?

Set 5

1. Which fibre grows on the seed of a variety of plants of the genus *Gossypium*?
2. What is the first letter of the Greek alphabet called?
3. In which present-day state is the historical site of Haldighati located?
4. Which Indian gallantry award literally means 'Wheel of the Ultimate Brave'?
5. More than 600 places in Australia are named after which flightless bird?
6. Was the film *Roja* first made in Hindi or Tamil?
7. What's the word?

MATHS AND IQ

1. How is Tanu's paternal grandfather's only sister's only brother's son related to Tanu?
2. Fill in the blanks with either addition, subtraction, multiplication or division to figure out the correct answer. Go sequentially from left to right without following BODMAS.

7		3		5		41	=	9

3. A man ate 100 mangoes in 5 days. Each day, if he ate 6 more than the previous day, how many did he eat the first day?
4. Fill in the blanks with either addition, subtraction,

multiplication or division to figure out the correct answer. Go sequentially from left to right without following BODMAS.

26		23		3		5	=	14

5. In a code language, 'poka beri' means 'fine cloth', 'meta sira' means 'clear water' and 'lona sira beri' means 'fine clear weather'. Which word in that language means 'weather'?

VOCABULARY

1. Rearrange the letters of the word 'DONE' to get a part of a plant.
2. Rearrange the letters of the word 'LURE' to get a word that means king's reign.
3. Rearrange the letters of the word 'ERASE' to get an Indian garment.
4. Rearrange the letters of the word LIAR to get the name of a place where wild animals live.
5. Read the word DRAW backward to mean sections in a hospital

SPEED

1. Tanuja is Kajol's sister, mother or aunt?
2. Who was introduced as Mickey Mouse's pet blood-hound in *The Chain Gang*?
3. The India Gate is in Mumbai: agree or disagree?
4. Is Pongal an important festival of Bihar or Tamil Nadu?
5. How many collars do thirty wet shirts have?

6. Who is the heroine of *Much Ado About Nothing*: Viola or Beatrice?
7. If the 1996 cricket World Cup was called the Wills World Cup, what were the World Cups of 1975, 1979 and 1983 called?
8. How long is a Guinea pig's tail?
9. Which reed did the ancient Egyptians make into a type of paper?
10. In cricket, a score of 0 is called a duck or a chicken?

ANSWERS

TAKE YOUR PICK

1. Orangutan
2. Clement Attlee
3. Persian Gulf
4. Indra
5. Lewis Carroll
6. Javed Akhtar
7. An African snake
8. W.G. Grace
9. Lata Mangeshkar
10. Khan Abdul Ghaffar Khan

WHAT'S THE QUESTION

1. Name different varieties of oranges.
2. What is enamel?
3. What is Barbie's full name?
4. Who is Govind Nihalani?
5. What is the meaning of the word 'astronaut'?
6. What is the name given to a portable loose-leaf notebook?
7. What is a shoe horn?
8. When was the walkman invented?
9. In summer, which hot, dry north Indian wind scorches the crops and grass?
10. What is a 'bit'?

MIXED BAG

1. Jordan
2. Uttar Pradesh
3. Beaver
4. Dibyendu Barua
5. Maharana Kumbha
6. Fahrenheit to Celsius
7. They are all diamonds.
8. Sir Winston Churchill
9. Poems
10. Shabana Azmi

SPOT THE ANSWER

1. A pond of frozen ice in a crater
2. Pyramids of Giza
3. Jim Corbett
4. On the birth of Indira Gandhi
5. Whether to break the broad or narrow end of an egg

CONFIDENCE ROUND

1. The Bahmani kingdom
2. Meerkat
3. Serious
4. Romania
5. *Macbeth*
6. Hot cross buns
7. Drive a car
8. Mussoorie

9. Taxis
10. Serious

WHAT'S THE WORD

Set 1

1. Dhow
2. Red
3. Apricot
4. Giraffe
5. Orville
6. New York City
7. DRAGON

Set 2

1. Red
2. Unicorn
3. Bees
4. Blue
6. Expand
6. Russia
7. RUBBER

Set 3

1. Puma
2. Ehsaan
3. Noddy
4. Chetan Sharma
5. India
6. Lotus
7. PENCIL

Set 4

1. Bihu
2. U-boat
3. Dennis Lillee
4. Ganesha
5. Elephant
6. Texas
7. BUDGET

Set 5

1. Cotton
2. Alpha
3. Rajasthan
4. Param Vir Chakra
5. Emu
6. Tamil
7. CARPET

MATHS AND IQ

1. Father
2.

7	Plus	3	Multiply	5	Minus	41	=	9

3. 2
4.

26	Minus	23	Multiply	3	Plus	5	=	14

5. Iona

VOCABULARY

1. NODE
2. RULE

3. SAREE
4. LAIR
5. WARD

SPEED

1. Mother
2. Pluto
3. Disagree. It is in New Delhi
4. Tamil Nadu
5. Thirty
6. Beatrice
7. Prudential Cup
8. It does not have a tail. It is not visible externally.
9. Papyrus
10. Duck

SET 16

TAKE YOUR PICK

1. Which is the only member of the cat family that hunts primarily during the day?
   a. Cheetah
   b. Lion
   c. Tiger

2. Which Portuguese explorer became a page to Queen Leonor, wife of John II, in Lisbon at an early age?
   a. Ferdinand Magellan
   b. Christopher Columbus
   c. Marco Polo

3. According to Hindu mythology, which was the second of the four yugas?
   a. Kali yuga
   b. Treta yuga
   c. Dvapara yuga

4. By what Indian name is 'sweet golden yoghurt' better known?
   a. Shrikhand
   b. Kheer
   c. Paneer

5. Which planet's most conspicuous feature is the Caloris Basin?
   a. Mars
   b. Jupiter
   c. Mercury

6. Which musical instrument did Guru Nanak's friend and companion Mardana play?
   a. Sitar
   b. Tanpura
   c. Rabab

7. Lake Kawaguchi is noted for reflecting the image of which mountain in its waters?
   a. Mount Fuji
   b. Mount Kilimanjaro
   c. Mount Etna

8. In which of these sports is the term 'fluke' most likely to be used?
   a. Billiards
   b. Football
   c. Hockey

9. Which gemstone is commonly judged by the 'four Cs': carat, clarity, colour and cut?
   a. Opal
   b. Diamond
   c. Amethyst

10. Which film starring Aishwarya Rai is based on

O. Henry's short story, *The Gift of the Magi*?
a. *Khaki*
b. *Bride and Prejudice*
c. *Raincoat*

WHAT'S THE QUESTION

1. Alexander Selkirk, a Scottish sailor, provided the inspiration for the story.
2. The group of twelve who decide if a person is guilty or innocent.
3. In the Mahabharata, she was Abhimanyu's mother.
4. It is the only country to have a non-rectangular or square flag.
5. The fattest of Robin Hood's merry men.
6. A game in which players buy and sell houses and hotels.
7. Mount Pidurutalagala is the highest point of this country.
8. This horizontal bone connects the shoulder blade and the sternum.
9. This machine's name comes from Latin, meaning 'to make similar'.
10. This Mughal emperor, the son of Shah Jahan, called himself Alamgir (world conqueror).

MIXED BAG

1. It lies in Australia and rises 335 metres abruptly from the sand dune plains, about 450 km from Alice Springs. It is perhaps the world's largest monolith.

What is it?

2. Who was the first Communist chief minister in India?

3. In 2001, whose record did Mohammed Ashraful of Bangladesh break, to become the youngest cricketer to score a Test century?

4. Which city would you be in if you passed under the famous Bridge of Sighs?

5. Who has published a book of poems and reflections titled *Dancing the Dream*?

6. Which historical place connects Ibrahim Lodi's battle against Babur in 1526, Akbar's victory over Hemu in 1556 and Ahmad Shah Abdali's conflict with the Marathas in 1761?

7. In 1864, who became a resident master in Elgin's Weston House Academy in Scotland?

8. Who is common to Dasher, Dancer, Prancer, Vixen, Comet, Cupid, Donner/Donder, Blitzen and Rudolph?

9. The Swiss Guards are responsible for the safety of which religious head?

10. 'Four legs good, two legs bad' is the essence of animalism as described in which book?

SPOT THE ANSWER

1. The Tibetans call it Chomolungma, meaning 'Goddess Mother of the World'. What is its English name?
   a. Yak
   b. Mount Everest
   c. Godwin-Austen or K2

2. Her native name was Ma Tint Tint. She later became Usha. Who was she?
   a. P.T. Usha
   b. India's former first lady Usha Narayanan
   c. Usha Mangeshkar

3. Where might you see Nishi warriors with hornbill caps and knives in monkey-skin scabbards?
   a. Russia
   b. Madhya Pradesh
   c. Arunachal Pradesh

4. In 1524, which famous explorer was buried in St Francis Church, Fort Kochi?
   a. Ferdinand Magellan
   b. Christopher Columbus
   c. Vasco da Gama

5. Traditionally, who uses a gold broom and acts as 'sweeper to the gods' at the Puri Rath Yatra?
   a. The head priest
   b. Gajapati Maharaja of Puri
   c. The chief minister of Odisha

CONFIDENCE ROUND

1. In tennis, which is the first Grand Slam tournament played in a calendar year: US Open or Australian Open?
2. Which is usually found underwater: a sloth or an oyster?

3. In Literature, the expression 'open sesame', is associated with: Aladdin or Ali Baba?
4. Who was the famous mother of Irene Joliot?
5. Who starred in the film *Khakee*: Amitabh Bachchan or Aamir Khan?
6. Which is the twin city of Hyderabad: Aurangabad or Secunderabad?
7. Which dance form originated in Kerala: Theyyam or Chhau?
8. Apart from 'Entry' which other signage starting with 'E' are you most likely to see inside a cinema?
9. Which Japanese military attack on 7 December 1941 was code-named Operation Z?
10. What number shirt did Pele wear during his football career?

WHAT'S THE WORD

Set 1

1. Give a three-letter word for a large, strong African antelope that has the Afrikaans name 'wildebeest'?
2. Pokhran is in which Indian state?
3. Which colour comes between yellow and red in a rainbow?
4. Which five letter word relates to a town or a city: urban or rural?
5. The Arctic Circle is near the North Pole or the South Pole?
6. Which cartoon duck celebrated his 80th birthday in 2014?
7. What's the word?

Set 2

1. Which is a closer relative of the giraffe: okapi or zebra?
2. The playing time of the full version of the Indian National Anthem is approximately how many seconds?
3. In the language panel of a contemporary banknote, in how many languages is its denomination written?
4. The name of which fabric literally means 'fasten, tie' in Malay: Ikat or Pashmina?
5. In America, the standard grid size of what is 15 by 15 squares for daily newspapers and 21 by 21 squares for Sunday editions?
6. Tiny bones called ossicles are part of which organ of your body?
7. What's the word?

Set 3

1. Who is the author of the book *The Athenian Constitution*: Socrates or Aristotle?
2. What is the highest number on a telephone keypad?
3. According to Lokmanya Tilak's famous slogan, what was his birthright?
4. In which state is Jaldapara Wildlife Sanctuary located?
5. The injury which is common in people who play a lot of tennis or other racquet sports is called tennis _____.
6. Which singer is famous for his song 'Bulla Ki Jana Main Kaun'?
7. What's the word?

Set 4

1. Which item of cutlery with prongs is also something you might come across on the road?
2. Shweta Nanda is the sister of which famous bollywood actor?
3. Which of these is a form of pasta: macaroni or semolina?
4. Which of these has Sachin Tendulkar played more of: Tests or One Day Internationals?
5. What is the capital of Mongolia?
6. What instrument does Ustad Hafiz Ali Khan's famous son play?
7. What's the word?

Set 5

1. Which famous Italian food item literally means 'pie': pasta or pizza?
2. Which animal has the largest brain of any land mammal: tiger or elephant?
3. Who has written the national anthem of Bangladesh?
4. Gandhinagar lies on the right bank of which river?
5. If *The Pickwick Papers* was Charles Dickens' first novel, which was his second?
6. In Hindu mythology, what is the name of Shiva's bull?
7. What's the word?

MATHS AND IQ

1. RAINBOW : WBIRANO : : ? : DAOLEPR
2. Fill in the blanks with either addition, subtraction, multiplication or division to figure out the correct

answer. Go sequentially from left to right without following BODMAS.

12		4		15		7	=	9

3. Fardeen likes to eat apples and oranges. Rintu likes to eat bananas and oranges, Anushua likes only oranges. Pritam eats only apples. Which fruit is liked by only one person?

4. Fill in the blanks with either addition, subtraction, multiplication or division to figure out the correct answer. Go sequentially from left to right without following BODMAS.

16		5		69		3	=	14

5. The first page of a book is on the right hand side and pages numbered 22 to 30 are missing. How many leaves have been torn out?

VOCABULARY

1. Rearrange the letters of the word 'SALE' to get the name of a famous lioness.
2. Rearrange the letters of the word 'LUMP' to get a fruit.
3. Rearrange the letters of the word 'MORE' to get a city.
4. Read the word 'FLOG' backward to get the name of a game.
5. Read the word 'LAP' backward to mean a friend.

SPEED

1. Which liquid do we generally have with cornflakes?
2. In 1901, who started a school at Shantiniketan named Bramhachari Ashram?
3. If Agatha Christie created Miss Marple, who created Hercule Poirot?
4. The Swiss flag consists of which two colours?
5. Who composed the music for the 1995 film *Rangeela*?
6. What is the STD code for Mumbai?
7. Where do women wear mascara?
8. *The Fellowship of the Ring* was initially published as the first part of which novel?
9. In which city is the Eden Gardens located?
10. The spacecraft Luna 2 landed on which celestial body?

ANSWERS

TAKE YOUR PICK

1. Cheetah
2. Ferdinand Magellan
3. Treta yuga
4. Shrikhand; indigenous to Maharashtra and Gujarat
5. Mercury
6. Rabab
7. Mount Fuji
8. Billiards
9. Diamond
10. *Raincoat*

WHAT'S THE QUESTION

1. Who inspired Daniel Defoe to write *Robinson Crusoe*?
2. What is a jury?
3. Who was Subhadra?
4. What is special about the flag of Nepal?
5. Who was Friar Tuck?
6. What is Monopoly?
7. What is Sri Lanka's highest point called?
8. What is the clavicle in the human body?
9. How did the fax machine get its name?
10. Who was Aurangzeb?

MIXED BAG

1. Ayers Rock
2. E.M.S. Namboodiripad
3. Mushtaq Mohammad, 17 years and 78 days
4. Venice
5. Michael Jackson
6. Panipat
7. Alexander Graham Bell
8. Santa Claus
9. The Pope
10. *Animal Farm* by George Orwell

SPOT THE ANSWER

1. Mount Everest
2. India's former first lady Usha Narayanan
3. Arunachal Pradesh
4. Vasco da Gama
5. Gajapati Maharaja of Puri

CONFIDENCE ROUND

1. Australian Open; it is usually played in the month of January.
2. An oyster
3. Ali Baba
4. Marie Curie
5. Amitabh Bachchan
6. Secunderabad
7. Theyyam

8. Exit
9. Pearl Harbour
10. Ten

WHAT'S THE WORD

Set 1
1. Gnu
2. Rajasthan
3. Orange
4. Urban
5. North Pole
6. Donald Duck
7. GROUND

Set 2
1. Okapi
2. Fifty-two
3. Fifteen
4. Ikat
5. Crossword
6. Ear
7. OFFICE

Set 3
1. Aristotle
2. Nine
3. Swaraj
4. West Bengal
5. Elbow
6. Rabbi Shergill

7. ANSWER

Set 4

1. Fork
2. Abhishek Bachchan
3. Macaroni
4. One Day Internationals
5. Ulaanbaatar
6. Sarod (Ustad Amjad Ali Khan)
7. FAMOUS

Set 5

1. Pizza
2. Elephant
3. Rabindranath Tagore
4. Sabarmati
5. *Oliver Twist*
6. Nandi
7. PERSON

MATHS AND IQ

1. LEOPARD

2.

12	Multiply	4	Plus	15	Divide	7	=	9

3. Banana

4.

16	Multiply	5	Minus	69	Plus	3	=	14

5. 5

VOCABULARY

1. ELSA

2. PLUM
3. ROME
4. GOLF
5. PAL

SPEED

1. Milk
2. Rabindranath Tagore
3. Agatha Christie
4. White and red
5. A.R. Rahman
6. 022
7. Eyes
8. *Lord of the Rings*
9. Kolkata
10. Moon

SET 17

1. The name of which breed of dog comes from a German word meaning 'splash in water'?
   a. Boxer
   b. Poodle
   c. Doberman

2. In Hindu mythology, who received the title of Indrajit after he defeated Indra in a battle?
   a. Vibhishana
   b. Meghnad
   c. Kumbhakarna

3. During his last days, who became the guardian of the ruler of Travancore?
   a. Raja Ravi Varma
   b. M.F. Hussain
   c. Jamini Roy

4. In 1982, the advent of colour television coincided with which event in India?
   a. First General Elections
   b. First Census
   c. Asian Games inauguration

5. In 1933, what name did Rabindranath Tagore choose for the baby of his secretary's daughter?
   a. Amartya
   b. Satyajit
   c. Kishore

6. What is the national tree of Pakistan?
   a. Deodar
   b. Peepal
   c. Cypress

7. Penne, bow and fusilli are different kinds of which tasty food item?
   a. Ice cream
   b. Cheese
   c. Pasta

8. What is the term used to describe an entertainer who makes a wooden dummy appear to speak?
   a. Puppeteer
   b. Veterinarian
   c. Ventriloquist

9. Which natural process gets its name from the Greek words meaning 'light' and 'together'?
   a. Evaporation
   b. Photosynthesis
   c. Respiration

10. *Krrish* is the sequel to which Bollywood blockbuster?
    a. *Koi Mil Gaya*

    b.   *Kabhi Khushi Kabhie Gham*

    c.   *Mission Kashmir*

WHAT'S THE QUESTION

1. This part of a radio is also called an aerial.
2. A mollusc with three hearts and eight arms.
3. Elephants use this for smelling, breathing, trumpeting, drinking and also to grab things.
4. In chess notation, this piece is designated as N.
5. Approximately, 78 per cent nitrogen, 21 per cent oxygen and 1 per cent other gases
6. The letters Q, U, X, Y and Z are never used in its naming by the World Meteorological Organization.
7. In the Ramayana, he was Bharata and Lakshmana's father.
8. Zambia gets its name from this waterbody.
9. The famous Calico Museum is located in this city.
10. This actor's original name was Shivaji Rao Gaekwad.

MIXED BAG

1. 'Checkpoint Charlie' was a checkpoint on the border of which two European cities? (Hint: The checkpoint no longer exists.)
2. What are you most likely to find inside a 'mermaid's purse'?
3. Who was the first recipient of the Rajiv Gandhi Khel Ratna Award?
4. In Einstein's equation $E=mc^2$, what does 'c' stand for?
5. The flag of which country depicts a crossed rifle and

hoe in black superimposed on an open white book?

6. Which US president adopted 'White House' as the official name of the Executive Mansion?

7. What was W.B. Yeats referring to when he said: 'I have carried the manuscripts of these translations around with me for days, reading it in trains or on the top of buses and in restaurants. I have often had to close it lest some stranger should see how much it moved me.'

8. Who was the first Indian woman to become the president of the Indian National Congress?

9. The Bimal Roy-directed film *Do Bigha Zamin* got its name from a poem by which famous author?

10. What was constructed by Emperor Akbar on the remains of an ancient site known as Badalgarh?

SPOT THE ANSWER

1. What is the difference between kajal and kohl?
   a. Kajal is for the eyelashes while kohl is for the eyebrows
   b. Kajal is for adults, kohl is for children
   c. There is no difference

2. According to Aristotle, what is the best provision for old age?
   a. Money
   b. Education
   c. Children

3. Which phrase is used to describe a prime minister's

inner cabinet or most trusted members?
a. Bedroom cabinet
b. Shower cabinet
c. Kitchen cabinet

4. Which children's novel by Dodie Smith is also a Walt Disney film?
   a. *The Little Mermaid*
   b. *The Lion King*
   c. *101 Dalmatians*

5. How is Kongzi better known to us?
   a. Confucius
   b. Dalai Lama
   c. Bruce Lee

CONFIDENCE ROUND

1. In which Shakespearean play would you meet Ariel, Prospero, Miranda and Caliban?
2. Which flavouring agent is called *banira* in Japanese?
3. Which is the first city to have hosted the Winter Olympic Games twice?
4. The Niagara Falls partly lies in: Canada or Mexico?
5. The deficiency of which element is the cause of the most common type of goitre?
6. Who wrote a treatise on geometry titled *Elements*: Euclid or Aristotle?
7. In which state is the Keoladeo National Park located?
8. Raj Ghat is the samadhi of which leader?
9. Which Indian philosopher started an ashram in

Puducherry: Sri Aurobindo or Ramanuja?

10. The Bara Imambara is in which Indian city: Panjim or Lucknow?

WHAT'S THE WORD

Set 1

1. Who composed the music for the film *Roja*?
2. In China, *mian pian* is a kind of noodle or boat?
3. With which classical dance form would you associate the name of Birju Maharaj?
4. Lao is the official language of which Asian country?
5. Which reddish-gray-coloured worm is often called a nightcrawler in the United States?
6. Mats Wilander was a world-class player in which sport?
7. What's the word?

Set 2

1. In the Ramayana, which demon was the eldest son of Vishravas and Kaikasi?
2. The brown bear and the Himalayan bear are both found in India. In which country would you find a koala bear in the wild?
3. Who played the title role in the 1959 film *Ben-Hur*?
4. Which danceform orginated in North India: Kathak or Kuchpudi?
5. In Indian football if the 'Red and Gold' is up against the 'Maroon and Green', then which two teams are playing?
6. In which Indian state is the Meenakshi Temple located?

7. What's the word?

Set 3

1. Are your vocal chords in your larynx or your trachea?
2. What is a wooden frame for holding an artist's work while it is being painted or drawn called?
3. In Norse mythology, Mjölnir is the hammer of which god of thunder and lightning?
4. Jan-Ove Waldner was professionally associated which indoor sport?
5. Which number does the Roman numeral XI represent?
6. Who is the author of the books *The Financial Expert and The Guide*?
7. What's the word?

Set 4

1. Elephant, harp and leopard are all species of which aquatic mammal?
2. Which of these countries is a member of SAARC: Pakistan or Germany?
3. Name the international township and study centre named after Sri Aurobindo Ghose in Puducherry.
4. In India, what happens on a national scale every ten years: census or elections?
5. The name of which planet is an English/German word meaning the 'ground'?
6. Which god, also known as Neelkantha, gave Parashurama his axe: Shiva or Brahma?
7. What's the word?

Set 5

1. In a rainbow, which colour comes between blue and yellow?
2. In *Asterix*, who fell into a cauldron of magic potion when he was a little boy?
3. Which shehnai player was born on 21 March 1916 in Bihar?
4. The duck-billed platypus and the echidna are the only two mammals to do what: lay eggs or fly?
5. What is the opposite of explosion?
6. Before 2006, how many planets were there in the solar system?
7. What's the word?

MATHS AND IQ

1. Amrita finished her work in 4 hours. Ahona finished her work in 400 minutes. Arunita finished her work in 1000 seconds. Who took the maximum time to finish her work?
2. Fill in the blanks with either addition, subtraction, multiplication or division to figure out the correct answer. Go sequentially from left to right without following BODMAS.

11		9		3		46	=	14

3. If the letters of the word ATMOSPHERIC are arranged alphabetically from left to right, which would be the first vowel from the right?
4. What number should logically replace the star in the following series: 4, 9, 25, 49, 121, *, 289?

5. Fill in the blanks with either addition, subtraction, multiplication or division to figure out the correct answer. Go sequentially from left to right without following BODMAS.

6		15		11		2	=	20

VOCABULARY

1. Rearrange the letters of the word 'MEAN' to get what people call you by.
2. Rearrange the letters of the word 'SLIDE' to get the name of a Hindi flim starring Shah Rukh Khan and Preity Zinta. (Hint: Two-word answer in Hindi.)
3. Rearrange the letters of the word 'BAKER' to mean separate into pieces.
4. Read the word 'MINED' backward to get he name of a fabric.
5. Read the word 'WAR' backward to get a word meaning uncooked.

SPEED

1. The Khajuraho temples are in Madhya Pradesh, Uttar Pradesh or Himachal Pradesh?
2. If your mother drinks black coffee, what would be missing from the coffee?
3. The name of which martial art was given by South Korean general Choi Hong-Hi: Tae kwon do, Sumo or Karate?
4. Who played a child actor in the film *Yadoon Ki Baraat:* Salman Khan or Aamir Khan?

5. How many degrees are there in a right angle?
6. Which planet was named after the messenger of the Roman gods?
7. An old-fashioned term for record player is called a gramophone or a turntable?
8. What is a mural painted on?
9. What is basmati a form of?
10. Teen Murti Bhavan in Delhi houses a museum in memory of which former prime minister?

ANSWERS

TAKE YOUR PICK

1. Poodle
2. Meghnad
3. Raja Ravi Varma
4. Asian Games inauguration
5. Amartya
6. Deodar
7. Pasta
8. Ventriloquist
9. Photosynthesis
10. *Koi Mil Gaya*

WHAT'S THE QUESTION

1. What is an antenna?
2. What is an octopus?
3. What does an elephant use its trunk for?
4. In chess, what is the knight also called?
5. What is the composition of air?
6. Which are the letters not used by the World Meteorological Organization in naming Atlantic hurricanes?
7. Who was Dasharatha?
8. The Zambezi River gives its name to which country?
9. What is Ahmedabad?

10. What is actor Rajnikanth's real name?

MIXED BAG

1. East Berlin and West Berlin
2. Eggs
3. Vishwanathan Anand
4. Speed of light in vacuum
5. Mozambique
6. Theodore Roosevelt
7. *Gitanjali* by Rabindranath Tagore
8. Sarojini Naidu
9. Rabindranath Tagore
10. Agra Fort

SPOT THE ANSWER

1. There is no difference.
2. Education
3. Kitchen cabinet
4. *101 Dalmatians*
5. Confucius

CONFIDENCE ROUND

1. *The Tempest*
2. Vanilla
3. St Moritz
4. Canada
5. Iodine
6. Euclid

7. Rajasthan
8. Mahatma Gandhi
9. Sri Aurobindo
10. Lucknow

WHAT'S THE WORD

Set 1

1. A.R. Rahman
2. Noodle
3. Kathak
4. Laos
5. Earthworm
6. Tennis
7. ANKLET

Set 2

1. Ravana
2. Australia
3. Charlton Heston
4. Kathak
5. East Bengal and Mohun Bagan
6. Tamil Nadu
7. RACKET

Set 3

1. Larynx
2. Easel
3. Thor
4. Table tennis
5. Eleven

6. R.K. Narayan
7. LETTER

Set 4

1. Seal
2. Pakistan
3. Auroville
4. Census
5. Earth
6. Shiva
7. SPACES

Set 5

1. Green
2. Obelix
3. Bismillah Khan
4. Lay eggs
5. Implosion
6. Nine
7. GOBLIN

MATHS AND IQ

1. Ahona

2.

11	Plus	9	Multiply	3	Minus	46	=	14

3. O

4. 169 (square of prime numbers)

5.

6	Plus	15	Minus	11	Multiply	2	=	20

VOCABULARY

1. NAME
2. *DIL SE*
3. BREAK
4. DENIM
5. RAW

SPEED

1. Madhya Pradesh
2. Milk
3. Tae kwon do
4. Aamir Khan
5. 90°
6. Mercury
7. Gramophone
8. Wall
9. Rice
10. Jawaharlal Nehru

SET 18

TAKE YOUR PICK

1. What is Black Widow a species of?
   a. Spider
   b. Cockroach
   c. Ant

2. A Rest of the World XI vs MCC match played at Lord's in 1987 was which Indian cricketer's last first-class match?
   a. Kapil Dev
   b. Ravi Shastri
   c. Sunil Gavaskar

3. In the Ramayana, who is Rama's sister?
   a. Urmila
   b. Kanta
   c. Shanta

4. In batik method of dyeing, patterned parts are traditionally covered with which substance so that they do not receive colour?
   a. Sugar
   b. Wax
   c. Salt

5. According to Acharya Vinoba Bhave, 'Spirituality + _____ = Sarvodaya'?
   a. Literature
   b. Science
   c. Politics

6. Which is the highest mountain peak outside Asia?
   a. Mount Kilimanjaro
   b. Mount Blanc
   c. Mount Aconcagua

7. Which work by Kalidasa recounts the legend of Rama's ancestors and descendants?
   a. *Meghadutam*
   b. *Vikramorvashi*
   c. *Raghuvansham*

8. Which of these vegetables forms the main ingredient of batata vada?
   a. Cauliflower
   b. Cabbage
   c. Potato

9. Who was the first Indian to win the Ramon Magsaysay Award?
   a. Acharya Vinoba Bhave
   b. Jawaharlal Nehru
   c. S. Radhakrishnan

10. Which fictional character has a boss named M, whose secretary is called Miss Moneypenny?

a.   Sherlock Holmes
b.   James Bond
c.   Clark Kent

WHAT'S THE QUESTION

1.   Peachick
2.   Sleet
3.   The leaves of this plant is used in the body-decorating process known as mehendi.
4.   He was the first chief minister of Andhra Pradesh.
5.   Raksha, a she-wolf, took care of him.
6.   This country was known as Ceylon.
7.   This word is a blend of the words smoke and fog.
8.   This ruler gave up warfare despite being victorious in the Kalinga War.
9.   It is the deepest lake in the world.
10.   Samta Sthal

MIXED BAG

1.   If you visited the Karni Mata Temple at Bikaner in Rajasthan, which animal or animals would you see being worshipped?
2.   Which town was known as Vatapi in ancient times and was the first capital of the Chalukya kings?
3.   Which is the only living species in the genus Struthio?
4.   Crisscross words is an earlier version of which board game?
5.   Shanti Van is the samadhi of which prime minister of India?

6. In the 1830s, what was marketed in the United States as Dr Miles's compound extract of tomato?

7. 'Yours is the Earth and everything that's in it, And—which is more—you'll be a Man, my son!' These are the last few lines of which poem?

8. Which word did Van Helmont invent to describe substances 'far more subtle or fine...than a vapour, mist, or distilled oiliness, although...many times thicker than air'?

9. Which overseas territory of the United Kingdom is also known as the Malvinas Islands?

10. Which famous Steven Spielberg film began with a woman being killed by a great white shark?

SPOT THE ANSWER

1. Which system of medical practice is based on 'like cures like'?
   a. Allopathy
   b. Acupuncture
   c. Homeopathy

2. What would you do with a tom yum?
   a. Play with it. It is a yo-yo.
   b. Climb it. It is the highest mountain in China.
   c. Eat it. It is a Thai soup.

3. Which tree did Tipu Sultan declare as a royal tree and monopolized its trade in 1792?
   a. Banyan
   b. Mango

    c.   Sandalwood

4. What is vellum, used for writing or printing on, made from?
    a.   Wood from the banyan tree
    b.   Animal skins
    c.   Wood from the eucalyptus tree

5. The name of which disease comes from a word in the Kimakonde language, meaning 'to become contorted', and describes the stooped appearance of sufferers?
    a.   Malaria
    b.   Chikungunya
    c.   Dengue

CONFIDENCE ROUND

1. In Hindu mythology, who is also known as Ganapati?
2. How many wisdom teeth do adult humans usually have: three, four, five or six?
3. Which colour is associated with the Dutch royal family: magenta or orange?
4. What did Omar Khayyam write: *Rubbaiyat* or *Shahmat*?
5. Which game in India is normally associated with 'tip cat': gilli danda or ludo?
6. Which is closer to Delhi: Bhopal or Hyderabad?
7. How many colours does the South African flag display?
8. Which novel by Emily Bronte revolves around Heathcliff and Edgar Linton?

9. Which is a positive word: Zindabad or Murdabad?
10. What is the principal ingredient of omelettes?

WHAT'S THE WORD

Set 1

1. In *Asterix*, who is also known as Troubadix in German?
2. What would you call a medium-sized sailing boat equipped for cruising or racing: coracle or yacht?
3. Which former cricketer was nicknamed 'Big C' or 'Hubert'?
4. If Lord Shiva's abode is Kailash, who stays at Vaikuntha: Lord Ganesha or Lord Vishnu?
5. What would you call an electronic version of a printed book?
6. Kudiyattam, performed by the Cakkayars of Kerala, is the only surviving theatre form in which language?
7. What's the word?

Set 2

1. Which legendary British king was the son of King Uther Pendragon?
2. Hing Kabuli Sufaid and Hing Lal are the two main varieties of asafoetida or fenugreek?
3. What does 'ra' in the abbreviation Radar stand for?
4. What is the official language of Egypt: Urdu or Arabic?
5. In terms of transport, what connects an autorickshaw and a tricycle: three wheels or three engines?
6. Which key on a standard keyboard is used to perform

various functions, such as executing a command or selecting options on a menu?

7. What's the word?

Set 3

1. *Open: An Autobiography* is written by which professional tennis player?
2. The name of which Union Territory means 'hundred thousand islands' in Sanskrit?
3. If you visited Arjuna's Penance, which temple town would you be in?
4. What is the name of the cat in the animated television series *Oggy and the Cockroaches*?
5. Which river in Central India was called Namade by the 2nd century Greek geographer Ptolemy?
6. Iraq was once the world's largest producer of date or coconut?
7. What's the word?

Set 4

1. What type of a fruit is an alphonso?
2. Which 1996 English film starring Arnold Schwarzenegger shares its name with a stationary item?
3. In English grammar, which word comes from a Latin word meaning 'name': phrase or noun?
4. Which cartoon duo's first cartoon together was called *Puss Gets the Boot*?
5. The name of which viscous liquid comes from the Latin word *oleum*?
6. Which animal is the zodiac sign of the constellation Aries?

7. What's the word?

Set 5

1. Which Indian did Han Jian lose to at the 1981 badminton World Cup final?
2. Which word describes a hundred thousand?
3. Which film actor connects *Lal Badshah*, *Agneepath* and *Sooryavansham*?
4. Which of these is an amphibian: newt or turtle?
5. What is the hard glossy substance that covers the crown of a tooth called?
6. M. Karunanidhi was the chief minister of which state in India?
7. What's the word?

MATHS AND IQ

1. At a meeting there were 1000 men. If 26 men out of every 50 wore black ties, how many did not wear black ties?
2. Fill in the blanks with either addition, subtraction, multiplication or division to figure out the correct answer. Go sequentially from left to right without following BODMAS.

8		5		4		32	=	20

3. One evening, just before sunset, Nisha and Nishant were talking to each other, face to face, on Nisha's terrace. If Nishant's shadow was exactly to the left of Nisha, which direction was Nishant facing?
4. Fill in the blanks with either addition, subtraction, multiplication or division to figure out the correct

answer. Go sequentially from left to right without following BODMAS.

| 60 | | 12 | | 3 | | 23 | = | 25 |

5. Which 3 letters will logically complete the series: ACF, GIL, MOR, _____ ?

VOCABULARY

1. Re-arrange the letters of the word 'ELBOW' to get the opposite of above.
2. Re-arrange the letters of the word 'VOTES' to get a kitchen appliance used for heating.
3. Re-arrange the letters of the word 'BAKE' to mean a bird's body part.
4. Read the word 'PETS' backward to mean an act of walking.
5. Read the word 'TEN' backward to get the name of a material used for catching fish.

SPEED

1. In which European country did Charles Lindbergh complete his transatlantic flight?
2. Exactly when did India get independence: midnight of August 14 or midnight of August 15?
3. Which is Delhi's best known observatory?
4. Which festival is celebrated on the same day as Narali Poornima or Coconut Day is in Maharashtra?
5. Is a kilogram more or less than a pound?
6. Was Athena a Greek goddess or a Roman goddess?

7. In which story would you find the Marquis of Carabas?

8. What four-letter word best describes the stitching on a cricket ball?

9. Who usually gets admitted into maternity wards: mummies, daddies or grandpas?

10. What was Phantom also known as: Mr Walker or Mr Runner?

ANSWERS

TAKE YOUR PICK

1. Spider
2. Sunil Gavaskar
3. Shanta
4. Wax
5. Science
6. Mount Aconcagua
7. *Raghuvansham*
8. Potato
9. Acharya Vinoba Bhave
10. James Bond

WHAT'S THE QUESTION

1. What is the baby of a peafowl called?
2. In Great Britain, what is the name for a wet mixture of snow and rain?
3. What is henna?
4. What was N. Sanjiva Reddy?
5. Who was Mowgli?
6. What is Sri Lanka?
7. What is smog?
8. Who was Ashoka?
9. Which is Lake Baikal?
10. What is the name of the samadhi of former Deputy

Prime Minister Jagjivan Ram?

MIXED BAG

1. Rats
2. Badami
3. Ostrich
4. Scrabble
5. Jawaharlal Nehru
6. Ketchup
7. *If* (by Rudyard Kipling)
8. Gas
9. Falkland Islands
10. *Jaws*

SPOT THE ANSWER

1. Homeopathy
2. Eat it. It is a Thai soup.
3. Sandalwood
4. Animal skins
5. Chikungunya

CONFIDENCE ROUND

1. Ganesha
2. Four
3. Orange
4. *Rubbaiyat*
5. Gilli danda
6. Bhopal

7. Six
8. *Wuthering Heights*
9. Zindabad
10. Egg

WHAT'S THE WORD

Set 1
1. Cacofonix
2. Yacht
3. Clive Lloyd
4. Lord Vishnu
5. E-book
6. Sanskrit
7. CYCLES

Set 2
1. King Arthur
2. Asafoetida
3. Radio
4. Arabic
5. Three wheels
6. Enter
7. KARATE

Set 3
1. Andre Agassi
2. Lakshadweep
3. Mahabalipuram in Tamil Nadu
4. Oggy
5. Narmada

6. Date
7. ALMOND

Set 4

1. Mango
2. *Eraser*
3. Noun
4. *Tom and Jerry* (Initially named Jasper and Jinx, only Tom was identified as Jasper onscreen.)
5. Oil
6. Ram
7. MENTOR

Set 5

1. Prakash Padukone
2. Lakh
3. Amitabh Bachchan
4. Newt
5. Enamel
6. Tamil Nadu
7. PLANET

MATHS AND IQ

1. 480
2.

8	Plus	5	Multiply	4	Minus	32	=	20

3. North
4.

60	Divide	12	Minus	3	Plus	23	=	25

5. SUX

VOCABULARY

1. BELOW
2. STOVE
3. BEAK
4. STEP
5. NET

SPEED

1. France
2. The midnight of August 14
3. Jantar Mantar
4. Raksha Bandhan
5. More. One kilogram is equal to 2.2 pounds.
6. Greek. Minerva is her Roman equivalnet.
7. *Puss in Boots*
8. Seam
9. Mummies
10. Mr Walker

SET 19

TAKE YOUR PICK

1. In International women's cricket, the first Test match won by India was against which team?
    a. England
    b. Australia
    c. West Indies

2. In Karnataka, a yakshagana performance starts and ends with a prayer to which god?
    a. Ganesha
    b. Rama
    c. Indra

3. What did Louis Braille lose while he was playing in his father's shop at the age of three?
    a. His teeth
    b. His sight
    c. His speech

4. Which river rises in the Black Forest mountains of western Germany and flows to the Black Sea?
    a. Danube
    b. Volga
    c. Rhine

5. In Hindu mythology, who is the god of death?
   a. Yama
   b. Indra
   c. Surya

6. Which famous English author was born in 1903 in Motihari in Bihar?
   a. George Orwell
   b. Rudyard Kipling
   c. Ruskin Bond

7. What is a tandoor oven traditionally made of?
   a. Wood
   b. Metal
   c. Clay

8. Who is a couch potato?
   a. A person who spends a great deal of time eating potato chips
   b. A person who spends a great deal of time watching television and exercising
   c. A person who spends a great deal of time watching television and almost no time exercising

9. What does 'M' in MRI stand for?
   a. Musical
   b. Magnetic
   c. Mirror

10. Which musician played the role of Inder Lal in the 1983 film *Heat and Dust*?

   a. U Srinivas
   b. Zakir Hussain
   c. Shiv Kumar Sharma

WHAT'S THE QUESTION

1. He wrote the book *Curries and Other Indian Dishes*.
2. Right Faith, Right Knowledge, Right Conduct
3. It is called Al-Bahr Al-Ahmar in Arabic.
4. In 1973, after eighteen years in exile, he was re-elected president of Argentina.
5. Baba Buddha was the first keeper of this religious book.
6. Sir Ronald Ross discovered it within the Anopheles mosquito in 1897.
7. It is usually divided into the Palaeolithic, Mesolithic and Neolithic Ages.
8. Their celebration is called a jamboree.
9. This unit of length, often used in reference to depth of water, is equal to six feet.
10. He was exiled on the island of Elba in 1814–15.

MIXED BAG

1. If Scotland is known for its bagpipes, what musical instrument is the national symbol of Ireland?
2. The hammer, anvil and stirrup are bones in which organ of the human body?
3. Which mountain peak is locally called Dapsang or Chogori?
4. Which national park is situated 14 km from Sawai

Madhopur and derives its name from the fort situated within its precincts?

5. Who built the famous Buland Darwaza to commemorate his victory in Gujarat?

6. In the 1984 parliamentary elections, which famous person did Madhavrao Scindia defeat in the Gwalior constituency?

7. What nickname is common to former cricketer Venkatapathy Raju and former tennis player Ken Rosewall?

8. What were sometimes called 'dissected maps' and were used to teach geography in England?

9. United States Patent No. 174465, issued in 1876, and recognized as the 'most valuable patent' was for what?

10. Who was the first actor to appear on the cover of *Time* magazine?

SPOT THE ANSWER

1. Which of these is another name for tea ceremony in Japan?
   a. Origami
   b. Bonsai
   c. Sado

2. In which novel by Charles Dickens would you meet Agnes Wickfield, James Steerforth and Clara Peggotty?
   a. *A Christmas Carol*
   b. *Oliver Twist*
   c. *David Copperfield*

3. How many milligrams make a kilogram?
   a. One thousand
   b. Ten thousand
   c. One million

4. With which sport would you associate the jumping style called Fosbury Flop?
   a. Long jump
   b. High jump
   c. Pole vault

5. Who among these was the son of a Pandava?
   a. Jatasura
   b. Ravana
   c. Ghatotkacha

CONFIDENCE ROUND

1. A person who studies rocks is called a rock star: serious or joking?
2. How much is two score and seven?
3. The opposite of manual is annual or automatic?
4. In I.C.S.E. and C.B.S.E., what does 'E' stand for?
5. Which affectionate term means zero in tennis?
6. In which continent is Spain located?
7. What is the main liquid in the English Channel?
8. Rajaraja I belonged to which dynasty: Cholas, Chalukyas or Hoysalas?
9. After which leader is the international airport of New Delhi named?
10. Is Patna on the Ganga or the Brahmaputra?

WHAT'S THE WORD

Set 1

1. Complete the name of this book by Roald Dahl: *Charlie and the ____ Factory*?
2. In which state of India is the Mount Abu Sanctuary located?
3. Which character did Amitabh Bachchan play in the film *Amar Akbar Anthony*?
4. Which unit of linear measure equal to 3 feet?
5. What is the study and treatment of tumours called?
6. The Empire State building in the US is named after the nickname of which state?
7. What's the word?

Set 2

1. Who gave the name Nivedita to Margaret Elizabeth Noble: Swami Vivekananda or Subhas Chandra Bose?
2. The name of which microscopic organism comes from the Sanskrit word *yas* which means 'to seethe or boil'?
3. According to mythology, what is the name of Krishna's chakra?
4. Siberian, Sumatran and Bengal are species of which animal?
5. Which disease is named after a river in the Democratic Republic of Congo (Zaire), near which the disease was first observed?
6. Which painter directed the film *Meenaxi: A Tale of Three Cities*?

7. What's the word?

Set 3

1. What is usually added to bread to make it rise?
2. Which is the home ground of the Bengal cricket team?
3. The name of which slow-growing plant comes from the Greek word *leikhēn*?
4. The museum, Madam Tussauds, is located in which city of England?
5. Which branch of medicine is concerned with the study and treatment of disorders and diseases of the eye?
6. Warszawa is another name of which city?
7. What's the word?

Set 4

1. In anthropology, which term is used to describe a member of any human group whose adult males grow to less than 150 cm (59 inches) in average height?
2. The name of which gemstone is said to be based on the Sanskrit word *upala* meaning 'precious stone'?
3. Canines and wisdom are types of what?
4. Amitabh Bachchan plays the role of the father in the film *Mahaan*. Who plays the role of his twin sons?
5. Which popular story by Robert Louis Stevenson was originally titled *The Sea Cook*?
6. Which is the largest city of Norway?
7. What's the word?

Set 5

1. In Hindi, it is called *bhaloo*. What is it called in English?

2. Who is the first prime minister since Pandit Jawaharlal Nehru to have become prime minister of India with two successive mandates?

3. Nocturnal animals are active during the day or night?

4. In the medical condition, jaundice, what colour does the skin or the whites of the eyes become?

5. Two Indian states have the same initials and end with the same seven-letter words. Name them.

6. Peter Pan fell out of his carriage and was taken to which fictional land?

7. What's the word?

MATHS AND IQ

1. Which number will logically replace the # sign in the following series: 4, 13, #, 193, 769, 3073?

2. Fill in the blanks with either addition, subtraction, multiplication or division to figure out the correct answer. Go sequentially from left to right without following BODMAS.

9		3		53		4	=	20

3. If today is Thursday, which day would be the day after tomorrow of the day before yesterday?

4. Fill in the blanks with either addition, subtraction, multiplication or division to figure out the correct answer. Go sequentially from left to right without following BODMAS.

45		30		5		3	=	25

5. Which letter should be added to RIDE to get the word denoting a group of lions?

VOCABULARY

1. Re-arrange the letters of the word 'SHELF' to mean something that the human body is made up of.
2. Re-arrange the letters of the word 'CHEATER' to mean a person who provides education for students.
3. Re-arrange the letters of the word 'LIFE' to get a folder or box for holding loose papers together.
4. Read the word 'KNITS' backward to mean something that emits a strong foul odour.
5. Read the word 'STAR' backward to get the name of a rodent.

SPEED

1. Nagaland is on the border of Bangladesh, Myanmar or Pakistan?
2. Plumage is the correct term for which part of a bird?
3. What is the capital of the Tibet Autonomous Region, southwestern China?
4. How many metres are there in 300 centimetres?
5. Which Indian-born footballer played for Bury Football Club in 2001?
6. The famous Pragati Maidan is situated in Bangalore, New Delhi or Chandigarh?
7. The recipients of the Victoria Cross are entitled to add which two letters after their name?
8. The inside of a spoon is convex or concave?
9. Who starred in the 1981 film *Umrao Jaan*: Rekha or Rakhee?
10. Which historical site is in present-day Pakistan: Taxila or Pataliputra?

ANSWERS

TAKE YOUR PICK

1. West Indies
2. Ganesha
3. His sight
4. Danube
5. Yama
6. George Orwell
7. Clay
8. A person who spends a great deal of time watching television and almost no time exercising.
9. Magnetic
10. Zakir Hussain

WHAT'S THE QUESTION

1. Who is Mulk Raj Anand?
2. What are the three jewels of Jainism?
3. What is the Arabic name of Red Sea?
4. Who was Juan Perón?
5. In 1604, who was appointed as the first keeper of the Guru Granth Sahib?
6. Who discovered the presence of the malarial parasite in the *Anopheles* mosquito?
7. Into what periods is the Stone Age divided?
8. What do you call a large rally by a group of Scouts?

9. What is a fathom?
10. Name the island on which Napoleon was exiled.

MIXED BAG

1. Harp
2. Ear
3. K2
4. Ranthambore National Park
5. Akbar
6. Atal Bihari Vajpayee
7. Muscles
8. Jigsaw puzzles
9. Telephone
10. Charlie Chaplin

SPOT THE ANSWER

1. Sado
2. *David Copperfield*
3. One million
4. High jump
5. Ghatotkacha

CONFIDENCE ROUND

1. Joking
2. 47
3. Automatic
4. Education
5. Love

6. Europe
7. Water
8. Cholas
9. Indira Gandhi
10. Ganga

WHAT'S THE WORD

Set 1

1. *Chocolate*
2. Rajasthan
3. Anthony Gonsalves
4. Yard
5. Oncology
5. New York
7. CRAYON

Set 2

1. Swami Vivekananda
2. Yeast
3. Sudarshan
4. Tiger
5. Ebola
6. M.F. Hussain
7. SYSTEM

Set 3

1. Yeast
2. Eden Gardens
3. Lichen
4. London

5. Ophthalmology
6. Warsaw
7. YELLOW

Set 4

1. Pygmy
2. Opal
3. Teeth
4. Amitabh Bachchan (He had a triple role.)
5. *Treasure Island*
6. Oslo
7. POTATO

Set 5

1. Bear
2. Atal Bihari Vajpayee
3. Night
4. Yellow
5. Andhra Pradesh and Arunachal Pradesh
6. Never Never Land
7. BANYAN

MATHS AND IQ

1. 49 (Each number in the series is the preceding number multiplied by 4 and then decreased by 3.)

2.

9	Multiply	3	Plus	53	Divide	4	=	20

3. Thursday

4.

45	Minus	30	Multiply	5	Divide	3	=	25

5. P

VOCABULARY

1. FLESH
2. TEACHER
3. FILE
4. STINK
5. RATS

SPEED

1. Myanmar
2. Feathers
3. Lhasa
4. Three
5. Bhaichung Bhutia
6. New Delhi
7. V.C.
8. Concave
9. Rekha
10. Taxila

SET 20

TAKE YOUR PICK

1. Which of these animals holds the record for having the largest brain in the world?
   a. Sperm whale
   b. Elephant
   c. Giraffe

2. Which of these cricket umpires also acted as a referee in a Football World Cup qualifying match?
   a. Steve Bucknor
   b. David Shepherd
   c. Dickie Bird

3. In ancient Rome, the warning 'cave canem' was meant for people to beware of which animal?
   a. Dog
   b. Cat
   c. Eagle

4. Which art form of Persia was introduced in Rajasthan under the patronage of Maharaja Sawai Ram Singhji?
   a. Batik
   b. Filigree
   c. Blue pottery

5. Which Indian state was known as the Lushai Hills District of Assam before it was renamed in 1954?
   a. Meghalaya
   b. Mizoram
   c. Nagaland

6. In Hindu mythology, who received the 'Brahma Sirastra' for saving Dronacharya's life?
   a. Bhima
   b. Arjuna
   c. Duryodhana

7. In which book would you come across the characters Mercedes and Abbe Faria?
   a. *Oliver Twist*
   b. *The Count of Monte Cristo*
   c. *Gulliver's Travels*

8. Which fruit was referred to as love apple by the French?
   a. Apple
   b. Cherry
   c. Tomato

9. What would a graphologist study?
   a. Handwriting
   b. Gemstones
   c. Birds

10. In which film would you meet these seven children: Liesl, Louisa, Friedrich, Kurt, Brigitta, Marta and

Gretl?
a. *Rapunzel*
b. *Mary Poppins*
c. *The Sound of Music*

WHAT'S THE QUESTION

1. Snowline
2. Moa is an extinct bird that was native to this country.
3. The first UN Secretary-General from Africa.
4. This dynasty was founded by a Chagatai Turkic prince named Babur.
5. Spun sugar on a stick
6. The flag of this country features the map of the country above two olive branches.
7. Trapezium
8. Yeti
9. Baht
10. In Hindi, it is known as *adrak*.

MIXED BAG

1. What is common to simple, greenstick, Pott's or impacted?
2. The famous Sun Temple of Modhera is located in which state?
3. Which observatory did Sawai Jai Singh build at Delhi, Jaipur, Varanasi, Mathura and Ujjain?
4. A hinny is a hybrid offspring of which two animals?
5. Set in the 1950s, which novel revolves around the fortunes of four families: the Mehras, the Kapoors,

the Khans and the Chatterjis?

6. What was the code name of the Indian operation in the Kargil war?

7. Which sportsman was once nicknamed 'The Louisville Lip'?

8. What does OMOV mean in terms of voting in many countries?

9. What part of a car engine is called a muffler in the US?

10. Who received the National Film Award for his debut role as a child artist in the film *Mera Naam Joker*?

SPOT THE ANSWER

1. Putrajaya is a city in...
   a. Malaysia
   b. Brunei
   c. Turkey

2. In which novel by Charles Dickens was the main character haunted by three spirits who took him to the past, present and future?
   a. *A Christmas Carol*
   b. *Oliver Twist*
   c. *David Copperfield*

3. The flightless bird rhea is native to which continent?
   a. Africa
   b. South America
   c. Asia

4. Which is the human body's biggest consumer of oxygen and the first organ to suffer if there is a shortage?
   a. Brain
   b. Kidney
   c. Heart

5. In 1813–14, Ranjit Singh, the king of Punjab, brought what back to India?
   a. Peacock Throne
   b. Koh-i-noor diamond
   c. His title

CONFIDENCE ROUND

1. Which is not a vertebrate: a python or a snail?
2. Maharashtra is the most populous state in India: serious or joking?
3. Which superhero's relative said: 'With great power comes great responsibility'?
4. What is a greenhouse made of?
5. What does the red circle on the Japanese flag represent?
6. Cinderella's coach was made from a guava: serious or joking?
7. Alphabetically, which country's capital comes earlier: Bangladesh or India?
8. In which sport is there a scrum: rugby or hockey?
9. Which water body is associated with the word 'Persian': bay or gulf?
10. Which epidemic in the 1300s in Europe got its name

from the black spots on the victims' bodies?

WHAT'S THE WORD

Set 1

1. The name of which desert is derived from *t'hul*, the general term for sand ridges?
2. Which gas protects the Earth from harmful ultraviolet rays?
3. What does 'U' in USB stand for?
4. Complete the proverb: Curiosity killed the _____.
5. Which is the study of the human skeleton: anatomy or astronomy?
6. By which name was the empress Mihr-un-nisa better known?
7. What's the word?

Set 2

1. The scientific name of which tree is *Azadirachta indica*: neem or peepal?
2. Kampala is the largest city of which country?
3. How is peppermint camphor better known?
4. Which word means 'One of the Majority' in Russian: Menshevik or Bolshevik?
5. What is the inflammation of the brain, caused by infection or an allergic reaction called: Encephalitis or Sinus?
6. Remy, a young rat, dreams of becoming a renowned French chef in which 2007 animated film?
7. What's the word?

Set 3

1. The fourteen coaches of which luxury train are named after former Rajput states?
2. The name of which country comes from the Equator which divides it unequally?
3. Which famous Kathak dancer founded a dance school named Kalashram: Pandit Birju Maharaj or Uday Shankar?
4. In Greek mythology, who opened a box and set free all evils?
5. As a department in a hospital, what does 'E' in the abbreviation ENT stand for?
6. The name of which animal comes from the Greek words for 'nose' and 'horn'?
7. What's the word?

Set 4

1. What is a flat paper container with a sealable flap, used to enclose a letter called?
2. Which independent emirate is located on the west coast of the Persian Gulf?
3. In the Ramayana, who was Lakshmana's wife?
4. Who played the female lead in the film *Aur Pyaar Ho Gaya*?
5. Which former Indian princely state lies between Assam, Mizoram and Bangladesh?
6. If kangaroo is one of the animals in the Australian Coat of Arms, which is the other?
7. What's the word?

Set 5

1. Who has been India's longest-serving prime minister?
2. If Vishakhapatnam is in Andhra Pradesh, in which state is Vijayawada?
3. Which famous monument is in Mumbai: Gateway of India or India Gate?
4. The original logo of which organisation was created by a team of designers, led by Oliver Lincoln Lundquist, in 1945?
5. In computers, what does 'A' in the abbreviation CAD stand for?
6. What is the correct geometric name of an equilateral parallelogram?
7. What's the word?

MATHS AND IQ

1. In the word RECTANGULAR, how many letters appear in the same positions as they do in the alphabet?
2. Fill in the blanks with either addition, subtraction, multiplication or division to figure out the correct answer. Go sequentially from left to right without following BODMAS.

8		6		12		1	=	5

3. I am a number between 20 and 40. One of my digits is half the other. The product of the digits is twice the sum of the digits. Which number am I?
4. Which is the odd one and why?
   PIUTEJR, TUARSN, PMLUATNI, NEENPUT

5. Fill in the blanks with either addition, subtraction, multiplication or division to figure out the correct answer. Go sequentially from left to right without following BODMAS.

15		4		20		22	=	25

VOCABULARY

1. Re-arrange the letters of the word 'CAUSE' to get a liquid substance served with food.
2. Re-arrange the letters of the word 'MARINE' to get a word meaning continue to exist.
3. Re-arrange the letters of the word 'HEART' to get the name of a planet.
4. Rearrange the letters of the word 'CHARM' to get the name of a month.
5. Read the word 'GEL' backward to get a part of the human body.

SPEED

1. Is tungsten a gas, liquid or metal?
2. On what surface is the French Open tennis tournament played?
3. Who is the first woman prime minister of India?
4. Which river flows through Washington DC?
5. Humayun was Akbar's father, grandfather or uncle?
6. What would you call a person who composes dance sequences in a film?
7. If Richie Rich applied for a passport, what would he

write under the surname column?

8. Karma Bhoomi is the memorial to Shankar Dayal Sharma or Jagjivan Ram?

9. What is the official language of Mexico?

10. What are you doing if your lachrymal glands are secreting liquid?

ANSWERS

TAKE YOUR PICK

1. Sperm whale
2. Steve Bucknor
3. Dog
4. Blue pottery
5. Mizoram
6. Arjuna
7. *The Count of Monte Cristo*
8. Tomato
9. Handwriting
10. *The Sound of Music*

WHAT'S THE QUESTION

1. What do you call the line on high mountains above which snow never melts?
2. What is New Zealand?
3. Who is Boutros Boutros-Ghali?
4. Who founded the Mughal dynasty?
5. What is candyfloss?
6. What is the flag of Cyprus?
7. In Great Britain, what do you call a four-sided plane figure with one pair of parallel sides?
8. What is another name for the Abominable Snowman?
9. What is the currency of Thailand?

10. What is ginger called in Hindi?

MIXED BAG

1. They are different types of fractures.
2. Gujarat
3. Jantar Mantar
4. A male horse and a female donkey
5. *A Suitable Boy* by Vikram Seth
6. Operation Vijay
7. Muhammad Ali
8. One Member One Vote
9. Silencer
10. Rishi Kapoor

SPOT THE ANSWER

1. Malaysia
2. *A Christmas Carol*. In the book, the miser Ebenezer Scrooge is visited by the Ghosts of Christmas Past, Present, and Yet to Come.
3. South America
4. Brain
5. Koh-i-noor diamond

CONFIDENCE ROUND

1. Snail
2. Joking. India's most populous state is Uttar Pradesh as on 23rd June, 2014.
3. Spider-Man

4. Glass
5. The sun
6. Joking; it was made from a pumpkin
7. Bangladesh
8. Rugby
9. Gulf
10. Black Death

WHAT'S THE WORD

Set 1

1. Thar
2. Ozone
3. Universal
4. Cat
5. Anatomy
6. Nur Jahan
7. TOUCAN

Set 2

1. Neem
2. Uganda
3. Menthol
4. Bolshevik
5. Encephalitis
6. *Ratatouille*
7. NUMBER

Set 3

1. Palace on Wheels
2. Ecuador

3. Pandit Birju Maharaj; Kalashram is in New Delhi
4. Pandora
5. Ear
6. Rhinoceros
7. PEPPER

Set 4

1. Envelope
2. Qatar
3. Urmila
4. Aishwarya Rai
5. Tripura
6. Emu
7. EQUATE

Set 5

1. Jawaharlal Nehru
2. Andhra Pradesh
3. Gateway of India
4. United Nations
5. Aided
6. Rhombus
7. JAGUAR

MATHS AND IQ

1. 2 (C, G)
2.

| 8 | Multiply | 6 | Divide | 12 | Plus | 1 | = | 5 |

3. 36
4. PMLUATNI (PLATINUM), others are names of planets: JUPITER, SATURN, NEPTUNE

5.

| 15 | Multiply | 4 | Divide | 20 | Plus | 22 | = | 25 |

VOCABULARY

1. SAUCE
2. REMAIN
3. EARTH
4. MARCH
5. LEG

SPEED

1. Metal
2. Clay
3. Indira Gandhi
4. Potomac River
5. Father
6. Choreographer
7. Rich
8. Shankar Dayal Sharma
9. Spanish
10. Crying

SET 21

TAKE YOUR PICK

1. Which creature is considered the most intelligent of all invertebrates?
   a. Starfish
   b. Box Jellyfish
   c. Common octopus

2. Of which international sporting event were Kaz, Ato and Nik mascots?
   a. FIFA World Cup 2002
   b. Winter Olympics 2002
   c. Summer Olympics 2000

3. With which food item does the legendary king, who presides over the carnival in Goa, share his name?
   a. Momo
   b. Thukpa
   c. Sushi

4. The oldest capital of which south Indian dynasty was Uraiyur (now Tiruchirappalli)?
   a. Chola
   b. Pandya
   c. Chera

5. In which of these states are you most likely to find the Chhotanagpur plateau?
    a. Tamil Nadu
    b. Jharkhand
    c. Maharashtra

6. On which musical instrument would you find 'syahi'?
    a. Sitar
    b. Tabla
    c. Flute

7. The treatise Tolkappiyam is the earliest existing theoretical work in which Indian language?
    a. Marathi
    b. Gujarati
    c. Tamil

8. In India, with which food item was Operation Flood associated?
    a. Sugar
    b. Milk
    c. Tea

9. The logo of which organization features a burning candle wrapped in barbed wire?
    a. Amnesty International
    b. Missionaries of Charity
    c. World Health Organization

10. In Hindu mythology, whose eighth son was named Devavrata?

a. Ambika
b. Ganga
c. Ambalika

WHAT'S THE QUESTION

1. The name of this animal means 'giraffe-necked' in the Somali language.
2. Another name for asteroids
3. This politician's father was the chief minister of Jammu and Kashmir between 1996 and 2002.
4. Starchy substance obtained from cassava roots
5. US portrait painter known for his dot-and-dash code system
6. In Hindu mythology, Ganga and Satyavati were his two wives.
7. A doughnut-shaped fried snack from southern India
8. Jungle Book's 'great grey lone wolf'
9. In India, it is also known as the 'Car Festival'.
10. It appeared on the Chinese flag till 1911.

MIXED BAG

1. With which organ of the human body would you associate the word 'renal'?
2. Who was the first recipient of the Dadasaheb Phalke Award?
3. *The Story of My Life* is the autobiography of the first non-Congress prime minister of independent India. Name him.
4. Which Asian country in the Pacific Ocean is made up

of 7,107 islands, the largest of them being Luzon?

5. Which bird has the largest eye of any land animal?

6. Name the mausoleum of Muhammad Adil Shah which distinctly echoes even the faintest whisper over ten times.

7. I have a brother named Mycroft. My character is based on the surgeon Dr Joseph Bell. I was created by Sir Arthur Conan Doyle. Who am I?

8. The name of which Indian percussion instrument literally means 'made of clay'?

9. What was the code name of the secret project to develop atomic bombs during World War II in the US?

10. Which German football player is credited with inventing the 'attacking sweeper' position?

SPOT THE ANSWER

1. In India, which of these notes does not have the special feature that helps the visually impaired to identify the denomination?
    a. ₹10
    b. ₹20
    c. ₹50

2. The name of which of these cities literally means 'the city of cut-stone'?
    a. Nalanda
    b. Kalinga
    c. Taxila

3. From the tears of which god is the rudraksha tree believed to have originated?
   a. Vishnu
   b. Shiva
   c. Brahma

4. In 1933, what was created by Hermann Goring from the political and espionage units of the police of the German state of Prussia?
   a. CIA
   b. Gestapo
   c. Buchenwald

5. The 'Srikalahasti' and 'Machalipatnam' styles of Kalamkari art originated in…
   a. West Bengal
   b. Andhra Pradesh
   c. Odisha

CONFIDENCE ROUND

1. Which director is common to the films *Mr India* and *Bandit Queen*?
2. What kind of birds provided early airmail services?
3. A cube has: four, six or eight faces?
4. A hinge joint joins your arm and shoulder: serious or joking?
5. Is Cherrapunji in Assam or Meghalaya?
6. Which is the first month in the Saka calendar?
7. In the Bible, who built an ark to save the animals?
8. Expand the acronym UFO.

9. The name of which character is a synonym for a miser: Scrooge or Fagin?

10. In a dictionary, what comes first: snow or sleet?

WHAT'S THE WORD

Set 1

1. Which city, located in Jharkhand, is considered to be India's first planned industrial city?

2. Around which part of your body would you wear a bajuband?

3. The superhero Batman is also known as the 'Caped Crusader' or 'the Man of Steel'?

4. Which word literally means 'empty orchestra' in Japanese?

5. Which short novel, one of the outstanding Christmas stories of modern literature, by Charles Dickens was originally published in 1843?

6. Which of these is located in Europe: Lebanon or Latvia?

7. What's the word?

Set 2

1. Pamulaparti Venkata were the first names of which prime minister of India?

2. Which actor connects the films : *Dil*, *Mann* and *Ghulam*: Aamir Khan or Salman Khan?

3. Who was referred to by the title Admiral of the Seven Seas?

4. What is the Indian variant of ice cream that is served with faluda?

5. What is the tidal mouth of a large river, where the tide meets the stream called?
6. Who does the cartoon cat Sylvester always try to catch and eat?
7. What's the word?

Set 3

1. How many years did Rip Van Winkle sleep?
2. Originally from Africa, which vegetable is also known as *bhindi* or lady's finger: okra or gumbo?
3. After which goddess in Norse mythology is Friday named?
4. A badger's burrow is called a sett. What do you call a hare's lair?
5. Aural polyps affect which organ of the human body?
6. Which keyboard key is commonly used to move the cursor to the bottom of the screen or file?
7. What's the word?

Set 4

1. Which actress became Miss India in 1984?
2. Grandmaster is the highest classification for a chess player. What is the classification immediately below it?
3. Sinus cavities are located in the bony skull of which sense organ?
4. Which spice is shaped like a bulb: garlic or ginger?
5. Which famous artist was known as 'Il Florentine' because he lived near Florence?
6. In which language did R.K. Narayan write his first novel?

7. What's the word?

Set 5

1. Which mythical animal appears on the flag of Bhutan?
2. What is the traditional Japanese art of paper folding called?
3. Which was established later: United Nations or League of Nations?
4. Which Mughal emperor was Umar Sheikh Mirza's son?
5. In the Ramayana, which city did Hanuman burn with the fire from his tail?
6. What is the point on the Earth's surface vertically above the focus of an earthquake called?
7. What's the word?

MATHS AND IQ

1. If A=1, B=2, C=3 and so on, what is the sum total of the consonants in the word MARCH?
2. Fill in the blanks with either addition, subtraction, multiplication or division to figure out the correct answer. Go sequentially from left to right without following BODMAS.

4		2		9		6	=	5

3. In a class, Geeta is sitting on Mita's left. Sita is sitting on Mita's right. Rita is sitting on Geeta's left. Arpita is sitting on Rita's left. Who is sitting on Geeta's right?
4. Fill in the blanks with either addition, subtraction,

multiplication or division to figure out the correct answer. Go sequentially from left to right without following BODMAS.

14		2		9		2	=	32

5. Which number will logically replace the # sign in the following series? 3, 6, 18, 72, #

VOCABULARY

1. Re-arrange the letters of the word 'PEA' to get the name of a primate without a tail.
2. Re-arrange the letters of the word 'PRESENT' to mean a large snake.
3. Re-arrange the letters of the word 'ICED' to mean a small cube used in games.
4. Read the word 'MOOR' backward to mean a space that can be occupied.
5. Read the word 'PACER' backward to mean state again.

SPEED

1. Name the author of the book *Malgudi Days*.
2. What is the most widely spoken language of Brazil?
3. Which royal title are some cobras given?
4. Ajmeri Gate, Kashmiri Gate and Turkman Gate are all located in which Indian city?
5. Which brothers flew the first plane: Wright, Wrong or Maybe?
6. Alexandria is the main port of which country?
7. What is dactyloscopy the science of?

8. What is the larva of a butterfly called?
9. Which one word describes track-and-field events?
10. Which city was formerly called Madinat-al-Salam or City of Peace in Arabic?

ANSWERS

TAKE YOUR PICK

1. Common octopus
2. FIFA World Cup 2002
3. Momo
4. Chola
5. Jharkhand
6. Tabla. Siyahi are the black spots on the tabla.
7. Tamil
8. Milk
9. Amnesty International
10. Ganga

WHAT'S THE QUESTION

1. What is a gerenuk?
2. What are planetoids?
3. Who is Omar Abdullah?
4. What is tapioca?
5. Who was Samuel Morse?
6. Who was King Shantanu?
7. What is a vada?
8. Who was Akela?
9. What is Rath Yatra?
10. What is a dragon?

MIXED BAG

1. Kidney
2. Devika Rani
3. Morarji Desai
4. The Philippines
5. Ostrich
6. Gol Gumbaz
7. Sherlock Holmes
8. Mridangam
9. Manhattan Project
10. Franz Beckenbauer

SPOT THE ANSWER

1. ₹10
2. Taxila
3. Shiva
4. Gestapo
5. Andhra Pradesh

CONFIDENCE ROUND

1. Shekhar Kapur
2. Pigeons
3. Six
4. Joking; it is a ball and socket joint
5. Meghalaya
6. Chaitra
7. Noah
8. Unidentified Flying Object

9. Scrooge
10. Sleet

WHAT'S THE WORD

Set 1

1. Jamshedpur
2. Arm
3. Caped Crusader
4. Karaoke
5. *A Christmas Carol*
6. Latvia
7. JACKAL

Set 2

1. P.V. Narasimha Rao
2. Aamir Khan
3. Christopher Columbus
4. Kulfi
5. Estuary
6. Tweety Pie
7. PACKET

Set 3

1. Twenty years
2. Okra
3. Frigg
4. Form
5. Ear
6. End
7. TOFFEE

Set 4

1. Juhi Chawla
2. International Master
3. Nose
4. Garlic
5. Leonardo da Vinci
6. English
7. JINGLE

Set 5

1. Dragon
2. Origami
3. United Nations
4. Babur
5. Lanka
6. Epicentre
7. DOUBLE

MATHS AND IQ

1. 42

2.

4	Divide	2	Plus	9	Minus	6	=	5

3. Mita

4.

14	Divide	2	Plus	9	Multiply	2	=	32

5. 360 (x2, x3, x4 etc)

VOCABULARY

1. APE
2. SERPENT

3. DICE
4. ROOM
5. RECAP

SPEED

1. R.K. Narayan
2. Portuguese
3. King
4. Delhi
5. Wright
6. Egypt
7. Fingerprint identification
8. A caterpillar
9. Athletics
10. Baghdad

SET 22

1. The name of which martial art form literally means 'art of kicking and punching' in Korean?
   a. Karate
   b. Sumo
   c. Tae Kwon Do

2. The name of which animal comes from a Spanish word meaning 'little armoured one'?
   a. Porcupine
   b. Armadillo
   c. Aardvark

3. What was adopted on 26 November 1949, but came into force on 26 January 1950?
   a. The Constitution of India
   b. The National Flag
   c. The State Emblem

4. Which famous historical city is situated on Sher Shah Suri Marg, 90 km from Delhi?
   a. Meerut
   b. Agra
   c. Panipat

5. In which system of therapy, also known as *shiatsu* in Japan, is the body divided into twelve main meridians?
   a. Reiki
   b. Acupressure
   c. Homeopathy

6. Which sea has often been called the incubator of Western civilization?
   a. Black Sea
   b. North Sea
   c. Mediterranean Sea

7. In which of these plants is the edible part called the 'tuber'?
   a. Potato
   b. Brinjal
   c. Onion

8. In 1939, the Ministry of Education of Taiwan designated whose birthday as Teachers' Day?
   a. Kublai Khan
   b. Confucius
   c. Fa Hien

9. As an offering to Krishna, every Brahmin or priest of the village of Kuchipudi is expected to perform which mythological character's role at least once in his life?
   a. Radha
   b. Rukmini
   c. Satyabhama

10. Nalappa's Mango Grove and Market Road are located in which fictional town?
    a. Malgudi
    b. Xanadu
    c. Dholakpur

WHAT'S THE QUESTION

1. Griffin's Wharf, Boston, 1773
2. It is the Russian word for 'fortress'.
3. He built a part of his own mausoleum (tomb) at Sikandra.
4. The Japanese word for 'tray planting'.
5. Domesticated ox-like mammal with shaggy hair sometimes called grunting ox.
6. Possibly the world's most popular sausage, also called wiener (Hint: German city).
7. It is also called dextrose.
8. The hero of Toyland
9. Yamunanagar is a district of this Indian state.
10. Dromedary and Bactrian

MIXED BAG

1. Name the music composer for the following films: *Pather Panchali, Aparajito* and *Apur Sansar.*
2. If they were not in your geometry book, where would you find your radius and ulna?
3. If you were admiring the Olive Ridley sea turtles on the Gahirmatha Beach, in which Indian state would you be?

4. Which word was included in the Oxford English Dictionary as a result of a sporting incident in 1932–33?

5. In which city was the first underground metro railway service in 1863?

6. In *Asterix and the Magic Carpet*, what was the name of the fakir on whose carpet Asterix and Obelix travelled to India?

7. The word 'Helvetia' appears on the stamps of which country?

8. The Apatanis are traditionally one of the most advanced weavers of which northeastern Indian state?

9. Which animals are the largest of South America's big cats?

10. Despite high temperatures, why do the filaments of light bulbs not burn?

SPOT THE ANSWER

1. *Sakuntala, The Miser, Lady with the Mirror* are some of the paintings of which famous painter?
   a. Jamini Roy
   b. Raja Ravi Varma
   c. M.F. Hussain

2. Which of these rivers features in *The Adventures of Tom Sawyer*?
   a. Nile
   b. Amazon
   c. Mississippi

3. If the president of India wishes to resign from his post, whom should he/she address the letter of resignation to?
    a. The vice president
    b. The prime minister
    c. The army chief

4. In Japanese, the name of which martial art form literally means 'way of harmonizing energy'?
    a. Tae kwon do
    b. Kung fu
    c. Aikido

5. What kind of animal is the 'kulan' that is generally found in the Gobi Desert?
    a. Wild camel
    b. Wild ass
    c. Armadillo

CONFIDENCE ROUND

1. With which cartoonist would you associate the *You Said It* series?
2. Which prime minister wrote *The Discovery of India*?
3. Who was the first cricketer to score four consecutive centuries in the ICC Cricket World Cup?
4. What kind of magnet can be switched on and off?
5. If Shah Jahan built the Taj Mahal, who built the Jama Masjid in Delhi?
6. The height of which animal is measured in 'hands'?
7. What are Garamond, Century and Verdana different types of: fonts or keyboard layouts?

8. Do we usually have one kidney or a pair of kidneys?
9. If Alice is to Wonderland, then Peter Pan is to what?
10. In Hindu mythology, who was also known as Panchali?

WHAT'S THE WORD

Set 1

1. Who created the famous detective Hercule Poirot?
2. In 1923, which country was founded by Kemal Ataturk?
3. Which fruit is called *zaitun* in Hindi?
4. Which actress was born as Begum Mahjabeen Bux?
5. Which god rides an elephant called Airavata?
6. A species of which plant is known as prickly pear?
7. What's the word?

Set 2

1. Mahendravarman I was the ruler of which dynasty?
2. The name of which element comes from a Greek word meaning 'violet coloured'?
3. '.ly' is the internet country code of which country in Africa?
4. Which is the largest gland in the human body?
5. In the film *Shrek*, what kind of a monster was Shrek?
6. The University of the District of Columbia is located in which city?
7. What's the word?

Set 3

1. The Bharat Ratna award is designed in the shape of which leaf?
2. What are walnuts called in Hindi?

3. In the world of literature, how is Rasipuram Krishnaswami Narayan better known?
4. In a film, if Shah Rukh Khan was G. One, Arjun Rampal was...
5. Barn, spectacled and snowy are different species of which bird?
6. Which country is divided into two parts called Thrace and Anatolia?
7. What's the word?

Set 4

1. Who became Miss World in 1994?
2. The *Man-Eater of Malgudi* is authored by which Indian writer?
3. In Hindu mythology, Shakuntala was the daughter of which apsara?
4. Which disease causes bones to become weak and brittle: osteoporosis or jaundice?
5. Which Indian tabla player was awarded the Padma Bhushan in 2002: Ustad Zakir Hussain or Pandit Kishan Maharaj?
6. Who was the famous Indian occupant of the spacecraft Soyuz T-11?
7. What's the word?

Set 5

1. In which country is Bastille Day a national holiday?
2. In ISP, if 'SP' stand for service provider, what does 'I' stand for?
3. Florence Nightingale is known as the Lady with the

4. Who is the author of *Ram Charit Manas*?
5. Which is the most important and oldest festival of the Christian Church, celebrating the resurrection of Christ: Christmas or Easter?
6. Lake Baikal, the deepest lake in the world, is located in which country?
7. What's the word?

MATHS AND IQ

1. Karishma decided to visit the museum. She is busy on Friday and Sunday. It is closed on Wednesday and Saturday. If she visits the museum on a weekday and after Tuesday, which day did she visit?
2. Fill in the blanks with either addition, subtraction, multiplication or division to figure out the correct answer. Go sequentially from left to right without following BODMAS.

15		6		3		4	=	28

3. Rita puts 4 apples in the first basket, 16 apples in the second basket, 36 apples in the third basket, and 64 apples in the fourth basket. If this pattern continues, how many apples will Rita put in the sixth basket?
4. Amrita thinks of a number. On subtracting 4 from 8 times the number, she gets 52. What is the number she originally thought of?
5. Fill in the blanks with either addition, subtraction, multiplication or division to figure out the correct answer. Go sequentially from left to right without following BODMAS.

23		6		13		5	=	6

VOCABULARY

1. Re-arrange the letters of the word 'DYNAMO' to get the name of a day of the week.
2. Re-arrange the letters of the word 'BOWL' to mean a powerful stroke with a hand.
3. Re-arrange the letters of the word 'AGREE' to mean anxious or impatient.
4. Read the word 'PAN' backward to mean sleep lightly.
5. Read the word 'DIAPER' backward to mean give back.

SPEED

1. Hydrogen sulphide gas smells of rotten bananas, eggs or meat?
2. What is the official language of Saudi Arabia?
3. What was the name for the dynasty of sultans who ruled from Delhi between 1026 and 1290?
4. Which two countries became one nation on 3 October 1990?
5. How many eggs does a peacock lay every two years?
6. The actress Manisha Koirala is from which neighbouring country?
7. Which word is common to an unmarried girl and an over in a cricket match in which no runs are recorded?
8. In which Indian state is Pune located?
9. The colour black is not in the rainbow: true or false?
10. The plural form of which word comes from the Greek word for 'mouth': stigmas or stomata?

ANSWERS

TAKE YOUR PICK

1. Tae Kwon Do
2. Armadillo
3. The Constitution of India
4. Panipat. Sher Shah Suri Marg is part of National Highway 1.
5. Acupressure
6. Mediterranean Sea
7. Potato
8. Confucius
9. Satyabhama
10. Malgudi

WHAT'S THE QUESTION

1. When and where did the Boston Tea Party take place?
2. What does the word 'kremlin' mean?
3. Who was Akbar?
4. What does 'bonsai' mean?
5. What is a yak?
6. What is a frankfurter?
7. What is glucose?
8. Who is Noddy?
9. Name a district of Haryana.
10. What are the two types of camels?

MIXED BAG

1. Pandit Ravi Shankar
2. In the human body. They are the bones of the forearm.
3. Odisha
4. Bodyline
5. London
6. Watziznehm or Kisasa
7. Switzerland
8. Arunachal Pradesh. Many tribes such as the Nyishis, Hill Miris, Akas, Buguns and Mijis depend on the Apatanis for their supply of cloth.
9. Jaguars
10. There is no air inside.

SPOT THE ANSWER

1. Raja Ravi Varma
2. Mississippi
3. The vice president
4. Aikido
5. Wild ass

CONFIDENCE ROUND

1. R.K. Laxman
2. Jawaharlal Nehru
3. Kumar Sangakkara
4. An electromagnet
5. Shah Jahan

6. The horse
7. Fonts
8. A pair
9. Neverland
10. Draupadi

WHAT'S THE WORD

Set 1
1. Agatha Christie
2. Turkey
3. Olive
4. Meena Kumari
5. Indra
6. Cactus
7. ATOMIC

Set 2
1. Pallava
2. Iodine
3. Libya
4. Liver
5. Ogre
6. Washington DC .
7. PILLOW

Set 3
1. Peepal
2. *Akhrot*
3. R.K. Narayan
4. Ra. One

5. Owl
6. Turkey
7. PARROT

Set 4

1. Aishwarya Rai
2. R.K. Narayan
3. Menaka
4. Osteoporosis
5. Ustad Zakir Hussain
6. Rakesh Sharma
7. ARMOUR

Set 5

1. France
2. Internet
3. Lamp
4. Tulsidas
5. Easter
6. Russia
7. FILTER

MATHS AND IQ

1. Thursday

2.

| 15 | Plus | 6 | Divide | 3 | Multiply | 4 | = | 28 |

3. 144 (square of 2, 4, 6 etc)

4. 56

5.

| 23 | Minus | 6 | Plus | 13 | Divide | 5 | = | 6 |

VOCABULARY

1. MONDAY
2. BLOW
3. EAGER
4. NAP
5. REPAID

SPEED

1. Eggs
2. Arabic
3. Slave Dynasty
4. East Germany and West Germany. They combined to form Germany.
5. None. A peacock does not lay eggs. It's the peahen which lays eggs.
6. Nepal
7. Maiden
8. Maharashtra
9. True
10. Stomata

SET 23

1. The name of which sport is believed to have come from a French word meaning 'shepherd's crook'?
   a. Hockey
   b. Golf
   c. Polo

2. Which of these breeds of dogs is also known as the plum pudding dog?
   a. Dalmatian
   b. Doberman
   c. Great Dane

3. Who launched the 'Bharat Jodo' or 'Knit India' movement from Kashmir to Kanyakumari in 1985?
   a. Baba Amte
   b. Sundarlal Bahuguna
   c. Mother Teresa

4. What is the name of a Japanese dish consisting of small balls or rolls of vinegar-flavoured cold rice served with a garnish of vegetables, egg or raw seafood?
   a. Falafel
   b. Tom yum
   c. Sushi

5. The name of which of these comes from a Greek word meaning 'without blood'?
   a. Anaemia
   b. Goitre
   c. Measles

6. What kind of a creature is Jerry in the cartoon series *Tom and Jerry*?
   a. Canary
   b. Cat
   c. Mouse

7. When produced before the magistrate, who gave his father's name as 'Swatantra' and his residence as 'prison'?
   a. Bhagat Singh
   b. Mangal Pandey
   c. Chandrashekhar Azad

8. Which mountain in Africa has three volcanic centres: Shira, Kibo and Mawenzi?
   a. Aconcagua
   b. Elbrus
   c. Kilimanjaro

9. Pichhwais, large paintings on cloth, depict legends from the life of which god?
   a. Ganesha
   b. Krishna
   c. Brahma

10. Who was born Hema but was later renamed after a character from her father's play *Bhaaw Bandhan*?
    a. Lata Mangeshkar
    b. Madhubala
    c. Nargis

WHAT'S THE QUESTION

1. Literally means 'great soul' in Hindi
2. This mountain is the major feature of Fuji-Hakone-Izu National Park.
3. 'Hum Sab Bharatiye Hain, Hum Sab Bharatiye Hain' is the song of this institution.
4. Acronym for 'Write Once Read Many'
5. The land of the Maori tribe
6. This event was also called the Amritsar Massacre.
7. Pituitary, thyroid and adrenal are some of these glands.
8. In Hindu mythology, he gave Saraswati her name.
9. Akbar's revenue minister who was also well known as Sher Shah's military engineer.
10. Sinhalese and Tamil are this country's two official languages.

MIXED BAG

1. Which cartoon character, part of the *Looney Tunes* series speaks only the two-word catchphrase, 'Beep Beep'?
2. What is a patty of minced beef, fried or grilled and typically served in a bread roll, and named after

Germany's largest port?

3. Which mountain was previously referred to as Peak XV by surveyors?

4. According to the most prevalent story, what mode of transport did Jonathan Scobie, an American missionary, invent in 1869?

5. In 1995, Christopher Pile or the Black Baron, was convicted of what?

6. In Tamil Nadu, who led the Salt Satyagraha March from Trichy to Vedaranyam on 13 April 1930?

7. What are brogue, clog and mule types of?

8. What is an OTC drug?

9. Which environment-concerned organisation was formerly called the 'Don't Make A Wave Committee'?

10. What word connects Eldorado, Bullion and California?

SPOT THE ANSWER

1. Which accessory could you buy using the measuring instrument Brannock device?
   a. Ring
   b. Shoe
   c. Trousers

2. Who was independent India's first education minister?
   a. Maulana Abul Kalam Azad
   b. Lala Lajpat Rai
   c. Atal Bihari Vajpayee

3. If you were living in Srinagar and a snowfall blocked your door, which common kitchen item would you use

to unblock it?
a. Salt
b. Sugar
c. Pepper

4. Which of these is the usual cause of devastating tidal waves called tsunamis?
    a. Solar eclipses
    b. Strong underwater earthquakes
    c. Aurora Borealis

5. According to Hindu mythology, which incarnation of Lord Vishnu killed all the male Kshatriyas on Earth, twenty-one successive times?
    a. Parashurama
    b. Kurma
    c. Bhima

CONFIDENCE ROUND

1. According to Newton's Third Law of Motion, what is there to every action?
2. What do antiques refer to?
3. A perimeter and boundary can mean the same thing: serious or joking?
4. Which part of a mint plant is used to make mint sauce?
5. How many of your forty-six chromosomes usually come from your mother?
6. During World War II, if Il Duce was Benito Mussolini, who was Der Führer?

7. Which is closer to Mumbai: Pune or Panaji?
8. Which folk art is from Bihar: Bidri or Madhubani?
9. Termites belong to a group of cellulose-eating insects: serious or joking?
10. How many minutes to 2 p.m. is it when it is 12.50 p.m.?

WHAT'S THE WORD

Set 1

1. In a game of cricket, what are bouncer, full length, and full toss: lengths of a delivery or speed of a delivery?
2. The layer of which allotrope of oxygen has gradually been depleted over Antarctica?
3. *Macavity's a Mystery* _____. What is the animal being spoken about in this poem by T.S. Eliot?
4. Land is measured in Katha or Thana?
5. What does the 'E' in UNESCO stand for?
6. Bronze, the first alloy was made by adding copper to which metal?
7. What's the word?

Set 2

1. The Hampi Dance Utsav is a major tourist attraction of which Indian state?
2. Who was the only daughter of Jawaharlal Nehru?
3. *With Time to Spare* is one of the autobiographies of which English left-handed batsman?
4. Which spice is a seed: nutmeg or clove?
5. What was the name of the smallest orphaned lioness in the 1966 film *Born Free*?

6. In which country was coffee first cultivated commercially: Yemen or Japan?
7. What's the word?

Set 3

1. In India, Jan Shatabdi, Jan Sadharan and Jan Sewa are types of what?
2. What does the letter 'U' stand for in 'URL', another name for a web-address?
3. In the world of entertainment, how is Enrique Martin Morales better known?
4. In the 11th century, Atisha Dipankar had preached which religion outside India: Buddhism or Sikhism?
5. Which mountain is often referred to as the spine of South America?
6. Around which part of the body would one usually wear a cravat?
7. What's the word?

Set 4

1. Maid Marian was the companion of which legendary outlaw hero?
2. In Jammu and Kashmir what are Ambri, American and Maharaji, varieties of?
3. If you had a late morning meal instead of breakfast and lunch, what would you have had?
4. If you were holidaying in Chittagong and Sylhet, in which country would you be?
5. If the letter 'P' in the abbreviation IP stands for protocol, what does the letter 'I' stand for?
6. In athletics, over how many days is the decathlon

spread?
7. What's the word?

Set 5

1. Which sport would you be playing if you represented your school in Subroto Mukherjee Cup?
2. Which city in Uttar Pradesh was founded by Sultan Sikandar of the Lodi dynasty in the early 16th century to be the capital of the Delhi sultanate?
3. Which six-letter word is common to a small portable computer, a medicine that you can swallow and a flat slab of stone?
4. If the Wright brothers are associated with an airplane, what are the Montgolfier brothers associated with: bicycle or hot-air balloon?
5. Considered to be the world's most expensive seafood, caviar is made from which part of a sturgeon fish?
6. If deforestation means the cutting down of trees, what is the replanting of trees called?
7. What's the word?

MATHS AND IQ

1. If Rani is twelfth from the right in a line of girls and fourth from the left, how many girls should be added to the line so that there are 20 girls in all?
2. Fill in the blanks with either addition, subtraction, multiplication or division to figure out the correct answer. Go sequentially from left to right without following BODMAS.

8		11		4		12	=	10

3. If you arrange the names of the planets of the solar system alphabetically, which planet would appear between Jupiter and Mercury?

4. Fill in the blanks with either addition, subtraction, multiplication or division to figure out the correct answer. Go sequentially from left to right without following BODMAS.

27		12		3		6	=	30

5. In a certain language if BASKET is written as TBEAKS, how is ORANGE written?

VOCABULARY

1. Re-arrange the letters of the word 'DONE' to a part of a plant.

2. Re-arrange the letters of the word 'RIPPLES' to mean a kind of shoe.

3. Re-arrange the letters of the word 'NOTICES' to mean distinct parts of division.

4. Read the word 'GEL' backward to get the name of a part of the human body.

5. Read the word 'GATEMAN' backward to mean a badge bearing the name of the wearer.

SPEED

1. Is Dover a British, French or American port?

2. Assuming he doesn't use blades or knives, what should a schoolboy use to sharpen a pencil?

3. What is the angular distance of a place east or west of the Greenwich meridian called: latitude or longitude?

4. In R.L. Stevenson's *Treasure Island*, what kind of bird is Captain Flint?
5. Which famous throne, commissioned by Shah Jahan, shares its name with a beautiful bird?
6. When iron reacts with the oxygen and water in moist air, it forms reddish - brown called...
7. Which film had the famous line , *'Kitney aadmi the'?'*
8. Which form of writing, popular in Egypt, translates literally to 'sacred carving' ?
9. If the Bullet Train is to Japan, then the TGV is to Germany, France or China?
10. What is the currency of Australia?

ANSWERS

TAKE YOUR PICK

1. Hockey
2. Dalmatian
3. Baba Amte
4. Sushi
5. Anaemia
6. Mouse
7. Chandrashekhar Azad
8. Kilimanjaro
9. Krishna
10. Lata Mangeshkar

WHAT'S THE QUESTION

1. What does the word 'Mahatma' mean?
2. What is Mount Fuji?
3. What is the NCC?
4. In computing, what is WORM?
5. What is New Zealand?
6. How is the 1919 Jallianwalla Bagh tragedy also known?
7. Name some endocrine glands in the human body.
8. Who is Lord Brahma?
9. Who was Raja Todar Mal?
10. Name the two official languages of Sri Lanka.

MIXED BAG

1. Road Runner
2. Hamburger (from Hamburg)
3. Mount Everest
4. The rickshaw
5. Writing a computer virus
6. C. Rajagopalachari
7. Shoes
8. Over-the-counter drugs. Medicines which are available without a prescription.
9. Greenpeace
10. Gold

SPOT THE ANSWER

1. Shoe
2. Maulana Abul Kalam Azad
3. Salt. When applied to snow or ice, salt lowers the melting point of the mixture.
4. Strong underwater earthquakes
5. Parashurama

CONFIDENCE ROUND

1. An equal and opposite reaction
2. Old things
3. Serious
4. Leaves
5. Twenty-three
6. Adolf Hitler

7. Pune
8. Madhubani
9. Serious
10. Seventy minutes

WHAT'S THE WORD

Set 1
1. Lengths of a delivery
2. Ozone
3. *Cat*
4. Katha
5. Education
6. Tin
7. LOCKET

Set 2
1. Karnataka
2. Indira Gandhi
3. David Gower
4. Nutmeg
5. Elsa
6. Yemen
7. KIDNEY

Set 3
1. Trains
2. Uniform (Uniform Resource Locator)
3. Ricky Martin
4. Buddhism
5. Andes

6. Neck
7. TURBAN

Set 4

1. Robin Hood
2. Apple
3. Brunch
4. Bangladesh
5. Internet
6. Two
7. RABBIT

Set 5

1. Football
2. Agra
3. Tablet
4. Hot-air balloon
5. Eggs
6. Reforestation
7. FATHER

MATHS AND IQ

1. 5
2.

| 8 | Multiply | 11 | Divide | 4 | Minus | 12 | = | 10 |

3. Mars
4.

| 27 | Minus | 12 | Divide | 3 | Multiply | 6 | = | 30 |

5. EOGRNA

VOCABULARY

1. NODE
2. SLIPPER
3. SECTION
4. LEG
5. NAME TAG

SPEED

1. British
2. Sharpener
3. Longitude
4. A parrot
5. Peacock
6. Rust or Iron Oxide
7. *Sholay*
8. Hieroglyphics
9. France
10. Australian Dollar

SET 24

TAKE YOUR PICK

1. Patients belonging to which blood group are said to be 'universal receivers'?
   a. O+
   b. B-
   c. AB+

2. On a standard computer keyboard, which of these keys has a left-pointing arrow on it?
   a. Caps Lock
   b. Enter
   c. Shift

3. The lines from which famous author's work adorns the players' entrance to Centre Court at Wimbledon?
   a. Rudyard Kipling
   b. William Wordsworth
   c. T.S. Eliot

4. Which insect is also known as 'white ant'?
   a. Honeybee
   b. Termite
   c. Mosquito

5. In which Indian state is the Surajkund Crafts Mela

held?
a. Punjab
b. Andhra Pradesh
c. Haryana

6. Originally known as Khadki or Khidki, which historical town in western India was founded by Malik Ambar in 1610?
a. Aurangabad
b. Kannauj
c. Udaipur

7. Who wrote the novels *Sevasadan*, *Rangamanch*, *Gaban*, *Nirmala* and *Godan*?
a. Munshi Premchand
b. Amrita Pritam
c. Mahasweta Devi

8. In cartoons, what tattoo does Popeye have on his forearm?
a. A spinach can
b. An anchor
c. A ship

9. Who was the last member of the Macedonian Ptolemaic dynasty to rule Egypt?
a. Cleopatra
b. Alexander
c. Nero

10. Tezpur chillies are named after an area in...

a. Nagaland
b. Assam
c. Rajasthan

WHAT'S THE QUESTION

1. According to the National Emblem of India, this animal is the guardian of the east.
2. This mathematical term means 'parts in each hundred'.
3. The name of this civilization in Greek means 'between rivers'.
4. This dance form of India was earlier known as sadir dasi attam.
5. Official office of the president of the United States
6. Second tallest land animal
7. Petruchio and Katherina (Hint: Literature)
8. This famous dog was created by Charles Monroe Schulz.
9. He has nephews named Morty and Ferdy.
10. The word comes from 'Sound Navigation and Ranging'.

MIXED BAG

1. In the film *Shrek Forever After*, who tricked Shrek into allowing himself to be erased from existence?
2. Which famous song, composed by Muhammad Iqbal, is also known as 'Tarana-e-Hindi'?
3. In comics, which small planetary body serves as home to the Norse gods such as Thor, and their ruler, Odin?

4. The capital of which African country is named after the US president James Monroe?

5. What kind of vehicle was sometimes referred to as 'Black Maria'?

6. What was carried in a third class train compartment numbered 2949 on 12 February 1948 to the Triveni, Allahabad?

7. The name of which animal comes from two Spanish words *el lagarto* meaning 'the lizard'?

8. In 1907, which scientist joined the Indian finance department as assistant accountant general?

9. Who was the first American author to submit a typewritten book manuscript?

10. What do you call a heavy tool for crushing things, typically in a mortar?

SPOT THE ANSWER

1. Which Indian was nominated for the Nobel Peace Prize in 1937, 1938, 1939, 1947 and 1948 but was never awarded the prize?
   a. Mahatma Gandhi
   b. Jawaharlal Nehru
   c. Sarvepalli Radhakrishnan

2. Which musical instrument is made up of the tumba, tabli and gulu?
   a. Tabla
   b. Sitar
   c. Piano

3. What is the main ingredient of shahi tukda?
   a. Bread pieces
   b. Cottage cheese
   c. Vermicelli

4. According to the nursery rhyme, after Jack fell down, whom did he run to for assistance?
   a. Old Man Top
   b. Old Dame Dob
   c. Mother Goose

5. In the Lok Sabha, which state has the highest number of seats?
   a. Maharashtra
   b. Uttar Pradesh
   c. West Bengal

CONFIDENCE ROUND

1. Gujarat shares a border with Madhya Pradesh: serious or joking?
2. Which planet became a dwarf planet in 2006?
3. Who erected twelve altars to the twelve Olympian gods on the Hyphasis, the present-day Beas?
4. Which colour shirt did the cricketers wear while playing in the first Cricket World Cup?
5. Norah Jones is the daughter of which musician?
6. In the binary system, which two digits represent all numbers?
7. Who wrote *Ritusamhara* and *Meghaduta*?
8. Which sitarist's debut film is *Dance Like a Man*?

9. Which is an Indian dessert: jalebi or zaffran?
10. In which present-day country was Gautama Buddha born?

WHAT'S THE WORD

Set 1

1. Commercially, what does the word 'aqua' refer to?
2. Razia Sultan was the daughter of which ruler?
3. In which country is Lumbini, the birthplace of the Lord Buddha located?
4. In a colony of bees, what are male bees called?
5. With which dance form is Kelucharan Mahapatra associated?
6. Tungsten has a single letter abbreviation on the periodic table. What is it?
7. What's the word?

Set 2

1. For contribution in which field is the Arjuna Award given?
2. What is the first hour of every sitting of the Lok Sabha called?
3. Who played the role of Miss Hawa Hawai in the 1998 film *Chhota Chetan*?
4. Who invaded Chittorgarh in 1303 to abduct Rani Padmini?
5. British chef William Harold described which sweet as 'a bowl of sweet, syrupy, soft cheese balls'?
6. Which mountaineer's autobiography is titled *Nothing Venture, Nothing Win*?

7. What's the word?

Set 3

1. What does the letter 'I' stand for in the name of the organisation FBI?
2. In Germany, this sign is called the 'Hakenkreuz'. What is it called in India?
3. The Great Sphinx at Giza in Egypt has a human head and the body of which animal?
4. Who lent her voice to the character Jewel in the 2011 film *Rio*?
5. Who, along with, Frederik Willem de Klerk was jointly awarded the Nobel Peace Prize of 1993?
6. What was the name of Hema Malini's horse in the 1975 film *Sholay*?
7. What's the word?

Set 4

1. Which famous author wrote under the pen name 'Boz'?
2. In which organ of the human body would you find bronchus?
3. In the national anthem of India, Odisha is referred to by which name?
4. Among many myths, Edward John Smith, the captain of which ship was known to ignore ice warnings?
5. Which country separates Alaska from most of the other states of the US?
6. What is the longest side of a right-angled triangle called?
7. What's the word?

Set 5

1. In which country is the Pre-Hispanic City of Chichen-Itza located?
2. What is the pigmented muscular curtain near the front of the eye called?
3. Which planet takes more than 100 years to complete one revolution: Mars or Neptune?
4. In 2014, which sportsperson played and won an exhibition cricket match against Yuvraj singh's team?
5. Which Navratna in Akbar's court is said to have created the ragas 'Miyan Malhar' and 'Miyan ki Todi'?
6. What is the line with 0° latitude called?
7. What's the word?

MATHS AND IQ

1. Ramesh opened a book and found that the sum of the two pages facing him was 221. What was the even number on one of the pages?
2. Fill in the blanks with either addition, subtraction, multiplication or division to figure out the correct answer. Go sequentially from left to right without following BODMAS.

42		6		9		3	=	13

3. If the letters of the alphabet are written from left to right, which letter is the sixth consonant from the right?
4. Fill in the blanks with either addition, subtraction, multiplication or division to figure out the correct answer. Go sequentially from left to right without

following BODMAS.

| 38 | | 25 | | 2 | | 4 | = | 30 |

5. If '<' means 'minus' and '>' means 'plus', '=' means 'multiplied by' and '$' means 'divided by', then what would be the value of 25>72$6<8

VOCABULARY

1. Rearrange the letters of the word 'TRAINER' to mean a stretch of land.
2. Rearrange the letters of the word 'THICKEN' to mean a room where food is cooked.
3. Rearrange the letters of the word 'REALTION' to mean something characteristic of Asia.
4. Read the word 'MAD' backwards to mean a barrier constructed to hold back water.
5. Read the word 'GARB' backward to mean say something in a boastful manner.

SPEED

1. The caves at Ellora belong to Buddhism, Jainism and which other religion?
2. If your parents celebrated their golden wedding anniversary, for how many years would they be married?
3. Jamshedpur is in Jharkhand, Bihar or Orissa?
4. In cricket, a batsman can be stumped off a wide ball: serious or joking?
5. Which number connects Ali Baba and Noah?
6. A popular medium on radio is FM. What does it stand

for?

7. Where is your thyroid gland located: throat or thalamus?

8. When it is summer in Sydney, Australia, what season is it in Delhi?

9. According to the nursery rhyme, what time was it when the mouse ran down?

10. Which green pigment found in plants is not present in fungi?

ANSWERS

TAKE YOUR PICK

1. AB+
2. Enter
3. Rudyard Kipling
4. Termite
5. Haryana
6. Aurangabad
7. Munshi Premchand
8. An anchor
9. Cleopatra
10. Assam

WHAT'S THE QUESTION

1. On the National Emblem, the elephant is the guardian of which direction?
2. What is per cent?
3. What does 'Mesopotamia' mean in Greek?
4. By what name was Bharatnatyam formerly known?
5. What is the Oval Office?
6. What is an elephant?
7. Name the two central characters in the Shakespearean play *The Taming of the Shrew*.
8. Who is Snoopy?
9. Who is Mickey Mouse?

10. What does SONAR stand for?

MIXED BAG

1. Rumpelstiltskin
2. 'Saare jahan se achcha'
3. Asgard
4. Liberia. The capital is Monrovia.
5. A police van
6. Mahatma Gandhi's ashes
7. Alligator
8. C.V. Raman
9. Mark Twain
10. Pestle

SPOT THE ANSWER

1. Mahatma Gandhi
2. Sitar
3. Bread pieces
4. Old Dame Dob
5. Uttar Pradesh

CONFIDENCE ROUND

1. Serious
2. Pluto
3. Alexander
4. White
5. Ravi Shankar
6. 0 and 1

7. Kalidasa
8. Anoushka Shankar
9. Jalebi
10. Nepal

WHAT'S THE WORD

Set 1

1. Water
2. Iltutmish
3. Nepal
4. Drones
5. Odissi
6. W
7. WINDOW

Set 2

1. Sports
2. Question Hour
3. Urmila Matondkar
4. Allaudin Khilji
5. Rasgulla
6. Edmund Hillary
7. SQUARE

Set 3

1. Investigation
2. Swastika
3. Lion
4. Anne Hathaway
5. Nelson Mandela

3. Dhanno
7. ISLAND

Set 4

1. Charles Dickens
2. Lung
3. Utkala
4. Titanic
5. Canada
6. Hypotenuse
7. CLUTCH

Set 5

1. Mexico
2. Iris
3. Neptune
4. Usain Bolt
5. Tansen
6. Equator
7. MINUTE

MATHS AND IQ

1. 110
2.

42	Divide	6	Plus	9	Minus	3	=	13

3. T
4.

38	Minus	25	Multiply	2	Plus	4	=	30

5. 29 (25 + 72 /6 - 8)

VOCABULARY

1. TERRAIN
2. KITCHEN
3. ORIENTAL
4. DAM
5. BRAG

SPEED

1. Hinduism
2. Fifty
3. Jharkhand
4. Serious
5. Forty
6. Frequency modulated
7. In your throat
8. Winter
9. One
10. Chlorophyll

SET 25

TAKE YOUR PICK

1. In the Mahabharata, under whose guidance was the lac palace built?
    a. Indrajit
    b. Sanjaya
    c. Purochana

2. Which of these tennis players is not of Belgian origin?
    a. Mary Pierce
    b. Kim Clijsters
    c. Justine Henin

3. In 79 CE, which natural disaster destroyed the cities of Herculaneum and Pompeii?
    a. Flooding of the Po River
    b. The eruption of the volcano Vesuvius
    c. Wildfire in the Botanical Garden of Padua

4. If '.in' is the Internet code of India, then '.zm' is the Internet code of which country?
    a. Zambia
    b. Zimbabwe
    c. South Africa

5. If your friends kept away from you because your axilla

was smelling, which part of the body would the axilla be?

a. Nose
b. Armpit
c. Feet

6. What was Kallu's profession in the 2002 film *Makdee*?
   a. Driver
   b. Butcher
   c. Greengrocer

7. Which bird has the largest known wingspan of any living bird?
   a. Peregrine falcon
   b. Albatross
   c. Ostrich

8. Which city in Uttarakhand would you go to if you want to attend the Kumbh Mela?
   a. Haridwar
   b. Dehra Dun
   c. Uttarkashi

9. On which famous landmark would you find the words 'Give me your tired, your poor, your huddled masses yearning to breathe free...'?
   a. The Statue of Liberty
   b. Eiffel Tower
   c. Qutb Minar

10. Which part of the body is affected by glaucoma?

    a. Feet
    b. Liver
    c. Eye

WHAT'S THE QUESTION

1. This elephant is the mascot of the Indian Railways.
2. 'Citius, Altius, Fortius' is the motto of these games.
3. He shifted his capital to Daulatabad in 1327.
4. 'An adventure 65 million years in the making' (Hint: Film)
5. This Belgian detective made his last appearance in the book *Curtain*.
6. The International Society for Krishna Consciousness
7. The first to enter all four pieces in the home square wins.
8. He murdered his brother Bleda in 445 CE to become a Hun ruler.
9. Stalinabad was the former name of the capital of this country.
10. A widely used email service co-founded by Sabeer Bhatia in 1996.

MIXED BAG

1. According to S. Radhakrishnan, which colour on the National Flag of India denotes our relation to soil and plant life?
2. With which traditional dress is an 'obi' worn?
3. In computer jargon, what does GIGO stand for?

4. Which Indian state was called North-East Frontier Agency till 1972?
5. In which country would you drive down an autobahn?
6. Which famous landmark was built in the thirteenth century by King Narasimhadeva in the shape of a chariot with twenty-four wheels, drawn by seven horses?
7. Which carnivorous mammal found in the Himalayan range is also called the ounce?
8. Alexander Graham Bell's notebook entry of 10 March 1876 describes the first successful experiment with which instrument?
9. 'There was no unkindness in Miss Marple, she just did not trust people.' This is a line from whose autobiography?
10. Who played the role of Wajid Ali Shah in the 1977 film *Shatranj Ke Khiladi*?

SPOT THE ANSWER

1. Which cricketer's first daughter is named after the Australian city Sydney?
   a. Shane Warne
   b. Brian Lara
   c. Ricky Ponting

2. Which of these is generally used to sterilize drinking water and to purify swimming pools?
   a. Iodine
   b. Chlorine
   c. Potassium

3. Who among these has represented India internationally in rugby for twenty-five years?
   a. Ashutosh Gowariker
   b. Rahul Bose
   c. Farhan Akhtar

4. In a calendar year, which is the only 31-day month that is followed by another 31-day month?
   a. June
   b. July
   c. August

5. On a Param Vir Chakra medal, the words 'Param Vir Chakra' are written in two languages. Which two?
   a. Hindi and English
   b. Hindi and Sanskrit
   c. Hindi and Tamil

CONFIDENCE ROUND

1. In which country would you find the temple of Preah Vihear?
2. Does a rhombus have three, four or five sides?
3. Who was lost in a cave with Becky Thatcher?
4. How many rings are there in the top row of the Olympic flag?
5. Which telephone sound can also be worn on the finger?
6. Most idlis are made from rice or wheat?
7. On what animal did Rani Lakshmibai do most of her fighting?

8. Which is the second largest ocean in terms of size?
9. Which disease is caused by *Salmonella typhi*?
10. What was the titular animal in the film *Flipper*?

WHAT'S THE WORD

Set 1

1. Which prime minister wrote a collection of poems called *Kaidi Kaviraj Ki Kundalian*?
2. In which Indian city would you be if you got down at the Egmore railway station?
3. The pollex is another name for which part of the human body?
4. The island of Sumatra belongs to which country?
5. According to Hindu mythology, who built the palace of Yama?
6. The loyalty of which character from *Winnie the Pooh* wins the hearts of his friends every time he loses his tail?
7. What's the word?

Set 2

1. Sheikh Hasina is an important leader of which country?
2. Which is the seventh planet from the sun?
3. Which of these comes from the Latin word for 'dog': canine or carmine?
4. How is the late singer/actor Abhas Kumar Ganguly better known?
5. *Panthera leo* is the scientific name of which animal?
6. Who is the elder daughter of King George VI and

Queen Elizabeth?

7. What's the word?

Set 3

1. Which is the largest country in North America in terms of area?

2. Whose diary was made into a play that premiered on Broadway in October 1955?

3. Whose famous painting is *The Syndics of the Clothmakers Guild*?

4. Which process, named after a French bacteriologist, prevents liquid food from getting spoilt?

5. In which part of the human body would you find stapes?

6. Which vegetable was referred to as pomodoro meaning 'golden apple' by the Italians?

7. What's the word?

Set 4

1. The elephant's tusk is made of ivory. What is a rhinoceros' horn made of?

2. Whose second novel, *The Luminaries*, won the 2013 Man Booker Prize?

3. In China, which ox-like mammal is known as 'hairy cattle'?

4. What is a single dot on a computer screen called?

5. *Manzana* is the Spanish word for which fruit or vegetable?

6. Which geographical feature shares its name with the fourth letter of the Greek alphabet?

7. What's the word?

Set 5

1. This city was known as Saigon until 1976. What is it called today?
2. Who is the only woman prime minister of India?
3. According to the nursery rhyme, who went up the hill with Jack?
4. Which fruit is also known by the name Indian Gooseberry: *amla* or *amrood*?
5. In the diagnostic tool ECG, what does the letter 'C' stand for?
6. Which king wrote *Amuktamalyada*?
7. What's the word?

MATHS AND IQ

1. My first three are in FEAR but not in FOUR, My fourth is in TAP but not in LAP. My last is in HEEL but not in FEEL. What am I?
2. Fill in the blanks with either addition, subtraction, multiplication or division to figure out the correct answer. Go sequentially from left to right without following BODMAS.

54		15		13		12	=	36

3. If you add all the even multiples of 7 appearing between 11 and 41, what will you get?
4. In a race, Joy was neither first nor last. Suraj beat Bobby, Tushar, and Joy. Suraj was neither first nor last. Rita beat Suraj. Who was first?
5. Fill in the blanks with either addition, subtraction, multiplication or division to figure out the correct

answer. Go sequentially from left to right without following **BODMAS**.

71		13		7		12	=	0

VOCABULARY

1. Rearrange the letters of the word 'FINGER' to mean the outer margin of an area.
2. Rearrange the letters of the word 'LASHES' to mean causing inconvenience.
3. Rearrange the letters of the word 'RESIN' to mean a device that makes a loud prolonged signal.
4. Read the word 'TUBED' backward to mean a person's first performance.
5. Read the word 'REBUT' backward to mean the underground part of a stem.

SPEED

1. If the cheetah is the fastest creature on four legs, which creature is the fastest on two legs?
2. Which of these is an official language of Canada: French or German?
3. A football goalkeeper is allowed to head the ball: yes or no?
4. What do we call the fourth month of the Gregorian calendar?
5. Which part of our body contains saliva: mouth or nose?
6. Who wrote the book, *The Man-eating Leopard of Rudraprayag*?

7. Which colour connects cobalt, prussian and navy?
8. With which Indian classical musical instrument is Pandit Ravi Shankar associated?
9. Which city would you visit in order to see the site of the bunker where Hitler died?
10. From January to December, Americans celebrate their Independence Day before or after India?

ANSWERS

TAKE YOUR PICK

1. Purochana
2. Mary Pierce
3. The eruption of the volcano Vesuvius
4. Zambia
5. Armpits
6. Butcher
7. Albatross
8. Haridwar
9. The Statue of Liberty
10. Eye. It is caused by an increase in pressure within the eyeball, causing gradual loss of sight.

WHAT'S THE QUESTION

1. Who is Bholu?
2. What is the motto of the Olympic Games?
3. Where did Muhammad Bin Tughlaq shift his capital?
4. What was the tagline for *Jurassic Park*?
5. Which was the last book to feature Hercule Poirot?
6. What is the full form of ISKCON?
7. How do you complete a game of Ludo?
8. Who was Attila?
9. What was the former name of the capital of Tajikistan?

10. What is Hotmail?

MIXED BAG

1. Green
2. Kimono
3. Garbage In, Garbage Out
4. Arunachal Pradesh
5. Germany
6. The Sun Temple, Konark
7. Snow leopard
8. Telephone
9. Agatha Christie
10. Amjad Khan

SPOT THE ANSWER

1. Brian Lara
2. Chlorine
3. Rahul Bose
4. July
5. Hindi and English

CONFIDENCE ROUND

1. Cambodia
2. Four
3. Tom Sawyer
4. Three
5. Ring
6. Rice

7. Horse
8. Atlantic Ocean
9. Typhoid
10. A dolphin

WHAT'S THE WORD

Set 1
1. Atal Bihari Vajpayee
2. Chennai
3. Thumb
4. Indonesia
5. Vishwakarma
6. Eeyore
7. ACTIVE

Set 2
1. Bangladesh
2. Uranus
3. Canine
4. Kishore Kumar
5. Lion
6. Elizabeth II
7. BUCKLE

Set 3
1. Canada
2. Anne Frank
3. Rembrandt
4. Pasteurization
5. Ear

6. Tomato
7. CARPET

Set 4

1. Keratin
2. Eleanor Catton
3. Yak
4. Pixel
5. Apple
6. Delta
7. KEYPAD

Set 5

1. Ho Chi Minh
2. Indira Gandhi
3. Jill
4. Amla
5. Cardio
6. Krishnadevaraya
7. HIJACK

MATHS AND IQ

1. EARTH

2.

54	Minus	15	Divide	13	Multiply	12	=	36

3. 98

4. Rita

5.

71	Plus	13	Divide	7	Minus	12	=	0

VOCABULARY

1. FRINGE
2. HASSLE
3. SIREN
4. DEBUT
5. TUBER

SPEED

1. Ostrich
2. French
3. Yes
4. April
5. Mouth
6. Jim Corbett
7. Blue
8. Sitar
9. Berlin
10. Before (July 4)